VOLVO
BUSES and COACHES

© 2016 Venture Publications Ltd

ISBN 978 1905 304 75 2

All rights reserved. Except for normal review purposes no part of this book may be reproduced or utilised in any form by any means, electrical or mechanical, including photocopying, recording or by an information storage and retrieval system, without the prior written consent of Venture Publications Ltd, Glossop, Derbyshire, SK13 8EH.

Front Cover
Lothian Buses has taken both double-deck and single-deck hybrid Volvos and No. 38, a Volvo 7900, one of 50, is shown crossing Dean Bridge on its way from Edinburgh city centre to the Ocean Terminal. (Mike Rhodes)

One of nine Plaxton Elite-bodied Volvo B11RT for trentbarton red arrow service that entered service in November 2015. Volvo had to fight off considerable opposition from other European manufacturers to win this order - a marked contrast to 40 years ago when the only competition came from Leyland. The striking livery was designed by Ray Stenning of Best Impressions. (PL)

VOLVO
BUSES and COACHES

FOUR DECADES OF CHANGE
and
DEVELOPMENT

Roger Carey

Venture *publications*

PHOTOGRAPHY

In 2014 Volvo revived its dormant relationship with Alexander's resulting in orders from both Stagecoach and Go-Ahead for the B5LH carrying the Alexander-Dennis NMM bodywork. This Stagecoach example is seen in Greenwich outside the Old Naval College in June 2015. With Transport for London demand for new vehicles reaching a peak in 2016 and 2017 Volvo anticipated a shortage of coach building capacity at its traditional partner, Wrights, and hence the need to offer not only A-D as a potential partner but also MCV in Egypt. (TQ)

The Author would like to thank the following photographers who have made this book possible. Their images are attributed by their initials, in addition to my own and those of STA, the extensive Senior Transport Archive, which holds a veritable treasure trove of material.

MB	Martin Bott	MJ	Michael Jeffries	TQ	Tony Quin
RC	Roger Carey	IL	Ian Longworth	ADS	Anthony Delaine Smith
DC	David Cole	PM	Peter Moore	ALS	AL Smith Collection
PC	Peter Coney	RM	Royston Morgan	STA	Senior Transport Archive
EL	East Lancs	KM	Kevin Moseley	JAS	John Senior
BE	Barry Edwards	HP	Harry Postlethwaite	DS	David Shaw
GNE	Go North East	SP	Stuart Pringle	JS	John Sinclair
DJ	Doug Jack	PL	Plaxton	VO	Volvo

CONTENTS

Chapter 1
Volvo buses and coaches come to the UK and Ireland — 7
  Opening the British Market to Volvo Coaches and Buses — 9
  Politics and Production — 17

Chapter 2
Volvo Coaches From the B58 to the B11R — 21
  B58 Coach Chassis — 22
  B10M Coach Chassis — 33
  B9M Coach Chassis — 54
  C10M Grand Touring Coach — 57
  Re-power With Volvo Engines — 59
  The Leyland Inheritance — 61
  Volvo and Express Operations
  National Express, Scottish Citylink, Stagecoach Express, Megabus and CIE — 65
  B12 Coach Chassis — 75
  B12M and B12B Coach Chassis — 78
  'Cabins' on Two and Three Axles — 88
  B7R Coach Chassis — 92
  B9R Coach Chassis — 96
  B11R Coach Chassis — 100
  B13R Coach Chassis — 102

Chapter 3
From the Ailsa to the B5LH — 103
  The Ailsa Double-deck Underframe — 104
  B59 Single-deck Chassis — 116
  Citybus Double-deck Chassis — 117
  B57 Chassis — 126
  B7M Single-deck Chassis — 128
  B10M Single-deck Bus Chassis — 129
  B6, B6LE and B6BLE Single-deck Chassis — 136
  B10L and B10LA Single-deck Chassis — 144
  B10B and B10BLE Single-deck Chassis — 148
  B7L and B7LA Chassis — 156
  B7RLE Single-deck Chassis — 162
  The Volvo Olympian — 168
  B7TL Double-deck Chassis — 174
  B9TL Double-deck Chassis — 180
  B5LH Double-deck Bus Chassis — 185
  7900 Hybrid Single-deck Bus — 188

Chapter 4
Euro 6 — 189

Chapter 5
The End Of The Road – Rust, Rescue, Restoration — 192

One of Arriva's Wright-bodied B5LH leaving the Shudehill Interchange in Manchester with a similar vehicle from the First Bus fleet behind. (JAS)

Chapter 1
Volvo buses and coaches come to the UK and Ireland

The story of how Jim McKelvie and Jim Keydon established Ailsa Bus in Barrhead, and later Irvine, in Scotland, has been very well told by Doug Jack in his volume 'The Volvo Bus'. However, in an era where emphasis is again being placed on entrepreneurship and small and medium enterprises, especially in engineering, it is a tale that is worth briefly recounting.

In 1945 Jim McKelvie took over the family haulage business and 20 years later had over 350 trucks, at which point he recognised the logic of big groups and sold out. With his experience of the British truck industry he decided to sell trucks – but with a difference. Unlike British products, chiefly from Leyland and AEC, the trucks he sold would be high specification. His company would have totally different attitudes to back-up service and treating customers and drivers as if they actually mattered – very little of which was to be found in Britain and British trucks in the late 1960s. McKelvie looked to Europe for the specification and attitude that he wanted. Jim Keydon managed the Pressed Steel plant at Linwood that, at that time, produced the body shells for the Volvo P1800 sports car. Keydon convinced McKelvie of the quality standards demanded by Volvo and McKelvie was, in turn, convinced that he had found the manufacturer he was seeking. McKelvie persuaded Volvo to sell him the F86 truck. McKelvie established a new company, Ailsa Trucks, and in 1967 the first F86 entered service in the UK. By 1973 Volvo claimed to have market leadership in the heavy truck sector. This was a very impressive track record and did not go unnoticed at the Volvo Bus Corporation that had been newly formed by Volvo in 1968.

Volvo had manufactured buses since the mid-1920s, but the early vehicles had been based on lorry chassis, giving a classic normal control vehicle. In 1934 the first purpose-built bus chassis appeared – the B1. There followed a range of chassis, all of which were front-engined. To produce an underfloor-engined vehicle required a horizontal engine, which Volvo did not have and could not afford to develop, even though the company recognised that this was the direction in which bus chassis, especially for Europe, were moving. By chance in the early 1960s the Swedish military were seeking a horizontal, turbocharged engine for a new range of tracked vehicles and put out a tender for the research and development of such an engine. Volvo won the tender and, at the expense of the Swedish military, reconfigured its newly developed, turbocharged vertical TD100 engine to a horizontal specification. Volvo now had an engine for a mid, underfloor-engined bus and coach. This has to be one of the more effective spin-offs from military R&D that has ever been produced.

With the newly developed horizontal engine, the B58 chassis was born. The chassis was well suited to bus work, with a low frame the saloon could be reached in three shallow steps. With a very low centre of gravity it was also suitable for high-floor touring coaches with adequate, underfloor luggage facility. By 1970 Volvo was keen to launch the B58 into the British market.

Whilst Volvo in Sweden were developing the horizontal version of the TD100 engine, in the UK there was a move away from the traditional front engine towards rear-engined double-deck vehicles. These new vehicles were proving to be mechanically very complex, unreliable, and prone to driver abuse as the engine was 'tucked away at the back'. The Scottish Bus Group, always a conservative organisation, had taken delivery of large batch of Bristol VRTs and, in a relatively short space of time, sent them all back south of the Border in exchange for more conventional Lodekkas. SBG made no secret of the fact that they preferred front-engined vehicles. After some prodding from Sweden, Jim McKelvie met with engineers from the SBG and the notion of modern front-engined vehicle began to take shape.

'What the industry said it wanted' – the ill-fated Guy Wulfrunian. It showed the way, but had too many problems and was put into production before many had been recognised and others resolved. Ailsa were able to take heed of these mistakes and the B55 chassis they produced became a long-lasting product. At the time of writing some B55s had clocked up over 35 years service and the last ones have only recently been withdrawn during the Summer of 2015. (JAS)

7

Sowerby's at Gilsland in North Yorkshire were early operators of part-used B58s. This example was new to Skill's at Nottingham. (MB)

The Ailsas delivered to Western SMT carried many liveries during their long lives. This example had been reseated by Western Buses with coach seats and liveried for the important No. 4 service from Glasgow to Ayr. (JS)

At the end of March 1971 Ailsa Trucks took the decision to develop a double-deck bus chassis. Guy Motors had already made an attempt to provide what the industry said it wanted with the Guy Wulfrunian. This used a heavy, bulky Gardner engine set to the offside at the front and had other innovations such as disc brakes. The Wulfrunian was not a success. Learning from Guy's errors, McKelvie used the compact, but powerful, TD70 engine (as used in the F70 truck he had so successfully introduced to GB), centrally mounted, but still allowing a perfectly adequate front entrance. The new chassis was to be built, with the approval of Volvo Sweden, at a new facility at Irvine, and it was given a Swedish designation, B55. Volvo was not altogether happy about having production undertaken of a vehicle to be Volvo badged being built outside the Volvo organisation, so, in order to remedy this problem, in 1972 they took a 75% holding in Ailsa Trucks.

Volvo were now equipped to launch into the British market. They had a single-deck chassis to offer for both bus and coach work; there was double-deck vehicle being developed and they held a 75% stake in the company that was to be responsible for the British and Irish market. The 1973 Scottish Motor Show at which Volvo launched its products was to lead to fundamental changes in the British bus and coach industry.

For three years following the 1973 launch, Jim McKelvie continued as the Managing Director, using all of his entrepreneurial flair to establish the Ailsa double-deck and the B58 coach chassis in the British market. He retired in 1976 and was replaced by Stig Arne Olsen who had the difficult task of sustaining the enthusiasm of the Ailsa Bus team whilst coping with the very depressed markets in the United Kingdom.

In 1977 Hugh Forrester, who had been Marketing Director of the new venture, left Ailsa Bus. It was decided to create a new post of General Manager. The post was filled by Sandy Glennie – an economist by training and a product of the Ford Motor Company graduate training programme. It is no exaggeration to say that this appointment revolutionised the British coach market especially, but also, over time, the bus market too – not to mention the position of Volvo in the UK and Irish markets.

Philosophically Sandy Glennie built on Jim McKelvie's notions that customers really mattered; that promises had to be kept; that delivery dates meant what they said; and that support and service was an integral part of the package. The

Sandy Glennie, retired and relaxed. For over 20 years from 1977 Sandy was the driving force behind the team that established Volvo as the brand leader in the UK and brought about major changes in the passenger vehicle distribution industry. (RC)

economist in Sandy Glennie also introduced new thinking for operators, especially the idea of whole life operating costs – that an expensive Volvo, a high quality product, giving greater reliability and durability, combined with a high residual value, was a much better buy than the initially cheaper competitor.

This thinking transformed the relationship between chassis manufacturer, bodybuilders, dealers and customers. From having to be persuaded to partner with Volvo the opposite became true – Volvo was the brand to which one had to be associated.

Opening the British Market to Volvo Coaches and Buses

1 – Buses

Ailsa Bus had developed the Ailsa double-deck underframe very much as an Ailsa Bus venture in collaboration with Walter Alexander and Scottish Bus Group. The result was a complete vehicle. To sell into the double-deck bus market it was, therefore, only necessary, formally, to respond to invitations to tender by the major operators who were the target market. Clearly much informal sales activity took place to convince Chief Engineers and other key players that the Ailsa was 'The right bus, at the right price, at the right time'. Independent operators – very few of whom bought new double-deck vehicles – would be offered vehicles to a major operators' specification which could be 'added on' to a production order – eg the two Van Hool McArdle-bodied Ailsas that were supplied to Tom Hunter in the A1 partnership.

A major obstacle that Ailsa Bus and its successors encountered was the proclivity of major municipal operators to 'buy local', almost irrespective of considerations of cost and reliability etc thus West Midlands purchased Daimlers, North Western municipalities almost universally bought Leylands and the Scottish Bus Group purchased almost exclusively Alexander-bodied vehicles. Despite the high British content of the Ailsa, and even the B10M with a UK-built body, this prejudice continued.

Volvo Trucks faced the same problem at a time when buying 'foreign', whatever its merits, was seen as being unpatriotic. Volvo addressed the issue in a variety of ways, the most important of which was to gain recognition by the Society of Motor Manufacturers and Traders as a British producer. This move was vociferously opposed by Leyland. Eventually the move was successful, and the argument became irrefutable once truck and bus production began at Irvine.

The Volvo marketing team actively looked at other ways of surmounting the perception of Volvo as 'foreign', one of the more enterprising being to badge vehicles as 'British Volvo' or, once Irvine was in production, as 'Scottish Volvo' reflecting the high UK sourced parts content and labour content of Volvo bus and coach products.

Ailsa Bus supplied very few single-deck bus-bodied B58s. This was very much a market testing operation and they were sold directly to the operators. In this process, Ailsa Bus took slots on the bodybuilder's production line and delivered a complete vehicle to the operator. In addition the UK Government Bus Grant Scheme, designed to allow small operators to renew their fleets, did lead to the production of a number of Bus Grant compliant B58 coaches that were used for stage carriage purposes.

With the advent of the B10M and specifically designed bus chassis the supply of single and double-deck vehicles has continued to be very largely controlled 'in house' with complete vehicles being supplied to the operator. As the range of products increased it was, of course, necessary to increase the sales effort with whole departments now devoted to bus sales. As always, there have been exceptions with a dealer taking a batch of perhaps 10 vehicles for supply to small operators needing one or two vehicles quickly – both Mistral and Southdown have sold small batches of B7RLE in this way.

Some initial 'roughs' of how Volvo might have branded itself had it not received recognition as a British manufacturer despite having a major supply chain in the UK. The opening of the Irvine factory resolved the issue.

2 – Coaches

A – the process

By 1973 Ailsa Bus Ltd had a problem. They had imported a right hand drive B58 chassis in late 1971 and wished to sell Volvo coach chassis into a market dominated by Leyland. Ailsa Bus had no partner bodybuilder, no agents, and no customers.

To start the process of acquiring all three, it had first to find bodybuilders willing to body Volvo chassis. This was easier said than done. Leyland dominated the heavyweight coach chassis market and had partnerships with both Duple and Plaxton who, in turn, dominated the UK market. It was easy for Leyland to 'lean on' those bodybuilders and suggest that it would be 'unwise' to take on Volvo.

Because of the impasse with Plaxton and Duple, and because Ailsa Bus had a good relationship with Walter Alexander in production of the Ailsa double-deck vehicle, the prototype B58 was bodied by Alexanders, not with a coach body, but with an Express-type body then very popular with the Scottish Bus Group. Ironically, although the Scottish Bus Group was a target market for Ailsa Bus Ltd, the prototype remained the only Alexander-bodied B58 for a number of years.

After some delay, and perhaps seeing the 'writing on the wall' for Leyland, and with a some pressure from Yeates, the dealer, both Plaxton and Duple agreed to body the B58 chassis for the 1974 season. Volvo, as the chassis manufacturer, supplied drawings etc to the bodybuilder and then supplied chassis through Ailsa Bus Ltd.

But 'small' coach operators purchase vehicles from dealers. Ailsa Bus had, therefore, to not only find bodybuilders but also had to find dealers willing to handle the Volvo products. This might have been very difficult but for the fact that Leyland was rationalising its range of vehicles – and the implication was that it would rationalise its dealer network too. Dealers who had been committed to Leyland for many years began to look to Volvo for their future.

Once appointed, the dealers had to find customers and place orders for both chassis and bodies. It was, and is, the dealer who brings these two components together and delivers the finished product to the customer. This is the key differentiation in selling coaches and buses in the UK market.

The coach sales effort, however, is a three sided one – Volvo and the bodybuilders and the dealers set out to convince a customer that their product is 'right for them'. To assist to familiarise potential users with the merits of the new product Ailsa Bus produced a number of demonstration vehicles which they would loan to would-be operators for varying periods – usually a few days, but sometimes for longer periods. Volvo would also hold 'Open Days' at Irvine and the premises of dealers to extol the virtues of the products that they wished to sell. This requires a great deal of co-operation, co-ordination and trust between the parties concerned. This process is aided by the fact that no-one gets paid until the coach is sold and paid for!

Volvo could also dangle the carrot of a visit to the Swedish bus factory at Boras where a group of selected customers could see their chassis being produced – and quite incidentally sample Swedish night life! It was difficult for Leyland to match this with night life in Preston!

A potential purchaser of a B58 coach, like his successor 40 years later, could either go to a dealer and specify precisely what was required and then wait a while whilst his or her bespoke package was put together. Or buy an 'off the shelf' product with the specification determined in all but minor matters by the dealer. Clearly, the former were very desirable customers, but the latter were no less important in shifting stock for dealers and the chassis importer.

'Large' or 'Fleet' operators enjoyed a slightly different process. They were able to deal directly with the chassis supplier and/or the bodybuilder. Fleet operators purchasing a number of identical vehicles might expect substantial

A B10M demonstrator leaves no doubt about its purpose! Kenzies managed to 'personalise' the vehicle by adding a sunshade. Kenzies became committed users of Volvo products for many years. Clearly a successful demonstration. (MB)

10

discounts on the 'list price' of new coaches. New vehicles would still be delivered through the dealer network, with the dealer carrying out pre-delivery checks etc.

B – the dealers

Initially dealers focussed on selling the new product. A key part of any dealer's activity, however, is the second hand market. It was important that prospective purchasers of new Volvo coaches were aware that the vehicle had a high residual value to justify the premium price he or she was paying in the first instance. The dealer played a key part in this process. And for the dealer it was important to ensure that there was a supply of good used vehicles to satisfy the operator who wanted a premium product but could not afford to purchase new, or who's business model was built around the purchase of sound used models.

In the 1970s most operators would seek finance for new purchases from their bank. But over the period of 40 years, dealers have become more important in financing sales through hire purchase, leasing and other arrangements. Very few operators write a cheque for the full value of the coach when taking delivery – a most notable exception being Glenton Tours who paid 'cash on the nail'! As supplying finance became an income stream in its own right to dealers, so Volvo also entered the finance market – sometimes offering a Volvo financial package through the dealer or sometimes independently. As in the car market, the provision of competitive financial products became part of the sales endeavour. Volvo led that way in educating bus and coach operators to learn that 'tax efficiency' was not something only for 'FT 100' companies.

Over a 40 year period Volvo has worked with a wide range of dealers. Dealers, however, have always been in an 'interesting' situation whereby the suppliers of both chassis and bodies wish to use their services and they can 'sell' these services to the highest bidder assuming that they felt the partnership could satisfy their own needs for profit etc. The most consistent Volvo coach dealer has been Yeates of Loughborough – the original dealer. Yeates, however, had a brief flirtation with Mercedes in the hope of increasing their bargaining power with Volvo. In 2000 Volvo paid Yeates the ultimate compliment and purchased the business, thereby moving to vertically integrate the coach sales business. This situation gives Volvo and much greater control over the quality of the product – and it keeps the dealer profit within the group.

By the early years of the 21st Century multi-franchise dealers were falling into decline as manufacturers purchased dealers – as Volvo did with Yeates – and they sold exclusively the manufacturers products. The exception to this is the Moseley Group, who, until Van Hool ceased to body chassis in 2013, were able to offer Van Hool-bodied Volvos alongside Bova and Van Hool integrals.

The move to vertical integration of sales and marketing has proceeded over the whole period since 1974 and Volvo now have a situation whereby they can offer an operator new and used coaches from a variety of bodybuilders through a Volvo owned dealership that can take used buses and coaches in part-exchange. Plaxton Coach Sales are the only other dealer offering Volvo chassis – unsurprisingly given the high proportion of Volvo coaches sold with Plaxton bodies. Both outlets can offer finance that will allow purchase, lease or contract hire and can include various levels of maintenance package.

OK Motor Services at Bishop Auckland operated this Duple-bodied B10M demonstrator. 'Small' operators, such as OK, usually had the use of a demonstrator for a few days only, or for a couple of weeks at most. Bodybuilders were naturally keen to have their products on such demonstration vehicles. (MB)

Demonstrators were important when introducing a new model, or, as with the Van Hool Astral, a new concept of a rear cabin. The driver's bunk (underneath the model name) and the large underfloor luggage capacity are evident on this photo taken at a Volvo Open Day at Irvine. (RC)

11

3 – Warranties

These are important documents. Initially a vehicle carried two warranties – one from Volvo for the chassis and one from the bodybuilder, for the body. This was a cumbersome process and open to dispute if something went wrong in the areas where body and chassis came into contact. With the increasing level of vertical integration in the industry it is now common for coaches and buses to have a 'whole vehicle' warranty. This is especially so for vehicles supplied by Volvo Coach Sales with Spanish-built Sunsundegui bodies or Volvo's own bodywork built in Poland.

4 – Spares and Maintenance

All vehicles require spare parts. Volvo supply original equipment specification spares as do the bodybuilders. Fitting non-Volvo parts can nullify a warranty. Dealers will carry a range of fast turnover spares but larger items will be supplied by Volvo, if necessary directly from Sweden. Speed of supply is critical. If an operator has invested a large sum of money in a new or second-hand vehicle it needs to be off the road for an absolute minimum of time. It was the strength of this support network that assisted Volvo to establish its position in the UK and Ireland, along with the availability of support from Volvo dealers across Europe for those operators venturing across the English channel.

It is also possible for larger operators, and those with a long history of Volvo operation, to hold a stock of impressed spares – usually of fast moving items. By this system, the parts are held by the operator and paid for as they are used.

Ailsa Trucks had built the Volvo truck reputation by appointing a number of key agents who not only sold Volvo trucks but also maintained them. These same truck dealers were also developed to service and maintain Volvo coaches. Traditionally, maintenance was almost universally carried out 'in house' by operators large and small, but with increasingly stringent health and safely regulations the notion of maintenance being carried out by a specialist – perhaps overnight when the vehicle was not needed – was one that became increasingly attractive. From a specialist carrying out maintenance it was a short step to the idea of contract maintenance, giving an operator a fixed cost to keep a vehicle on the road. This was revolutionary in the 1970s, even though it is common place today. Contract maintenance became very popular with bus fleet operators at times when skilled mechanics were in short supply.

VOLVO Dealers

(A) – the historical situation

Dealer	Year	Bodies
Yeates	1974	Plaxton, Duple, LAG, (Purchased by Volvo 2000)
Stanley Hughes	1974	Plaxton, Duple
Baker-West	1975	Plaxton, Duple.
Moseley	1975	Van Hool (Spanish-built on B58, Belgian-built thereafter) Caetano, Unicar
Kirkby	1979	Ajokki, Ikarus, Plaxton, Duple
Kirkby/Kingsforth	1979	Plaxton, Duple
John de Costa	1979	Irizar Urko only
Roeslare	1980	Jonckheere
Rydale	1981	Plaxton
Ensign	1982	Berkhof, Padane
Cotter	1982	Van Hool
Tramontana	1984	Irizar Pyrenean
Arlington	1987	Plaxton, Duple
S + N Glasgow	1988	Plaxton

(B) – the current situation

Dealer	Bodies
Volvo Coach Sales	Plaxton, Jonckheere, Sunsundegui, Volvo
Plaxton Coach Sales	Plaxton
Caetano/National Express	Caetano

Demonstration vehicles are usually built to the very highest standard to demonstrate all the 'bells and whistles' that are available. They are, therefore, popular purchases when their demonstration life is over - usually after a period of six to twelve months. Caelloi Motors at Pwllheli opted to keep the demonstration livery when it purchased this B10M/Duple Goldliner vehicle. (MB)

By contrast, Berrys at Taunton, repainted CNS 541X into their more restrained livery. Clearly finding the vehicles suitable for their rather different operations, both Berry and Caelloi remained loyal Volvo customers for many years. (DC)

Buses tend to have a longer life in demonstration mode, largely because operators want to test them for longer periods. This East Lancs-bodied Citybus spent over two years as a demonstrator before being sold to a member of the A1 Co-operative that ran past the door of the Volvo factory at Irvine. The adornments to the white livery indicate Volvo's support for the Bus and Coach Council and also emphasise the flat floor – though the number of potential passengers seems slightly exaggerated. (VO)

Low-floor and disabled access were emphasised on the graphics on the side of this B6BLE Wright vehicle. Whilst manufacturers competed to demonstrate the low-floor characteristics of their new products this form of raising public awareness was quite popular. (STA)

A more restrained message was given on the cove panels of the B10L demonstrator, seen here on loan to Timeline Travel of Bolton, but again illustrating the themes of 'modernity' and access for all. This photograph is unusual in that the Saffle System 2000' construction of the bodywork, along with the Ultra name, were also featured. Both features were removed at an early stage of the vehicle's demonstration career. (MB)

The demonstration of the B7TL to Dublin Bus, above, must be regarded as one of the more successful activities of this kind as Dublin Bus went on to operate almost 650 of these chassis. (MB)

Demonstrators tend to 'get around a bit', none more so than the B10B/Northern Counties demonstrator K247 HKV, seen left. It was used to demonstrate to both large and small operators. An example of the former is the visit it paid to Ulsterbus where it operated for Citybus in Belfast. (MB)

Amongst the smaller operators it was used by Your Bus in Birmingham, at that time competing with West Midland Travel in South Birmingham. Once demonstration life ended it was purchased by National Express and put to work on its Travel Dundee network, as seen below left and right. (DC both)

14

For dealers, the part-used market is very important. This is especially so for ex-London double-deck vehicles returning from lease with over five years of useful life left. The school bus market is especially important with local authorities now specifying low-floor vehicles and with a maximum of 15 year life. An East Lancs-bodied B7TL awaits a purchaser at Volvo Coach Sales. (DC)

Coaches tend to change hands more frequently, with major operators often seeing five years as a maximum for front-line touring service. Vale of Llangollen Travel took full advantage of this and acquired this ex-Trathen Berkhof-bodied B10M. The use of a personalised numberplate disguises the age of the vehicle. (MB)

Coaches from the fleet of Parks at Hamilton are eagerly sought by a wide range of operators. Bailiss at Barton-in-the-Beans in Leicestershire purchased this distinctive vehicle from that source. Located close to the field of the Battle of Bosworth, Bailliss' vehicles carried distinctive and partisan names and standards. (DC)

15

High-specification touring coaches, usually with relatively low mileage, are attractive purchases. McGill's use this ex-Wallace Arnold coach for express duties between Glasgow and Dunoon – including a ferry crossing. The air conditioning has been taken out of service. The separate radiators for the engine (forward) and intercooler are clearly visible. (RC)

Gibsons at Moffat in the Scottish borders were pleased to take this ex-Trathen B58/Plaxton Viewmaster for several years of rather less arduous, but still front line, service. For a small operator a good, part-used Volvo with excellent support service, made good business sense. (DC)

An interesting, and obviously very successful, business model has been followed by Downs at Mary Tavey near Tavistock in Devon. They have long followed the strategy of buying carefully selected used Volvo coaches, beginning with B58s and continuing through B10M and now with B12B. The entire full size fleet of 19 coaches has been acquired in this way. Jonckheere-bodied B10M Y7 CJD, seen here receiving a valet in the company's yard, began life with Parks of Hamilton. (RC)

Facing page:
Deregulation in Scotland led a number of enterprising operators to start long distance services and this was especially so in the north of the country. Nicolson's used this B10M/Van Hool to compete with the Scottish Bus Group. (MB)

Politics and Production

The bus industry, more than most, is 'dabbled in' by politicians of all shades. With a few very notable exceptions, most politicians, whether in Westminster or Brussels, display a considerable ignorance of what they are talking about. They have little thought for the consequence of their actions on the industry that produces buses and coaches – only for the headlines that they can make, sometimes for personal glory sometimes for ideological reasons.

During the 40 years that Volvo have been supplying the British market there have been a number of 'initiatives' from both Westminster and Brussels that have impacted on the manufacturing industry.

(a) – Great Britain

Domestically, perhaps one of the most important was the decision – taken before Ailsa Bus was even conceived – to take the very profitable Leyland Trucks and use it as the basis for a British automotive industry, linking it to the British car industry in a manner that was, ultimately, to prove fatal for the whole UK industry. From the formation of British Leyland Motor Holdings out of the British Motor Corporation almost all substantial investment went into the car division which continued to haemorrhage funding – to the detriment of Leyland and the companies that it had absorbed – AEC, Daimler and Bristol as well as the Eastern Coach Works. New products were developed 'on the cheap' and more slowly than should have been the case. Much of the development work was left to customers – who found to their cost that products were underdeveloped.

In order to make this behemoth work, and spurred on by ideological considerations, the Labour Government at Westminster decided to take control of the bus industry by two means – creating the National Bus Company to merge the British Electric Traction Group with the Tilling Group, the latter already in state ownership, and by establishing Passenger Transport Executives for the major conurbations, thereby abolishing municipal control of local bus services. In turn, NBC was to have a major shareholding in the Leyland division of the British Motor Holdings. This led to the creation of the 'one bus fits all' scenario of the Leyland National and the building of the vast new bus plant at Workington, in rural West Cumbria, far from both suppliers and customers, in order to provide employment in an area of rapid industrial decline. This development posed a severe threat to traditional chassis building at Leyland and Bristol and to all the bus bodybuilders.

This same Labour Government had determined that the average age of the British bus fleet was becoming too elderly, and had introduced a New Bus Grant scheme, whereby up to 50% of the cost of a new bus could be recouped from Government. Whitehall, of course, knows best and specified in some considerable detail what vehicles would, and would not, qualify for a bus grant. With an essential element being one person operation, the traditional front-engined, rear platform vehicle was no longer acceptable. This scheme was initially very helpful to the manufacturing industry, especially Leyland and Daimler, but like all subsidies, once it was reduced and finally withdrawn in 1984 the result was to depress demand for new vehicles. Volvo was only marginally affected as it did not offer a single-deck bus chassis at this time and only a few B58s received Plaxton 'Express' specification coachwork that qualified for the grant that was already declining.

Once in power again in 1983 the Conservative Government determined – again for largely ideological reasons – to undo the earlier control of the industry and produced probably the most major change in the industry since it had been created.

The 'Buses' White Paper of July 1984 made a number of far reaching proposals. In theory this was a discussion paper, but given the large majority that the Conservative Party had in Parliament, realistically, it was not likely to be altered very much in legislative form. The White Paper proposed; first, that Road Service Licensing would be abolished – de-regulation. This took away from the Traffic Commissioners the control of services whereby the Commissioners had taken cognisance of the existing provision and sought some evidence of demand before granting a new licence. Second, services were not be subsidised unless via a tendering process – this took away cross subsidisation of 'thin' routes from profitable routes. Third, the PTEs were to be stripped of their operating powers and power over NBC services within the PTE areas. Fourth, PTE operations, and the remaining municipal operations, had to be placed in stand-alone companies which were then to be prepared for sale. Fifth, the NBC and SBG were to be broken-up into units suitable for sale, and then sold; and finally taxis were to be allowed to carry passengers at individual fares. The White Paper led to the 1985 Transport Bill which passed in July of that year and became law in October 1985. Implementation took place on 26th October 1986.

For an industry that had been regulated in one form or another for over 50 years this was revolution indeed. No one in the industry had experience of operating in a de-regulated environment. Managers who had been concerned to satisfy regulators in one form or another now had to become entrepreneurial. The comfortable world of regulation had to make way for competition. Subsidies had to be replaced by profits. Like it or hate it this was transformational!

Almost immediately PTEs and the major bus companies ceased to buy new vehicles. As Leyland was the major supplier to these companies the impact was dramatic – and weakened an already struggling company further. Within a short period, this was to lead to Volvo taking over the Leyland bus and coach operation. In the short term Volvo was less affected as its main customers at that time were either the smaller, independent

17

coach operators who knew their local market and remained unaffected, or the touring and holiday groups that were equally unaffected. Indeed, deregulation of the express market led to a small fillip in demand by new operators 'dipping their toe in the water' – eg Morris Bros of Swansea and the formation of the British Coach consortium to offer long distance express services in competition to National Express.

The deregulation of the more local and urban services led to considerable innovation and the extensive use of high frequency minibuses to compete with the more staid offering of the established operator. Once more, this period of upheaval severely reduced demand for full-size vehicles.

Over-arching all of these considerations was the state of the British and Irish economy. For much of the early period of Volvo's involvement in the UK and Ireland the economy was in a weak state. This particularly affected the purchase of buses by both nationalised and private operators.

Given all of these factors the demise of chassis makers AEC, Daimler and Bristol was not surprising, nor the closure of bus bodybuilders Massey Brothers, Northern Counties, Willowbrook and ECW. None could survive in the parlous world of wildly fluctuating demand. Leyland was also terminally weakened and was purchased, first by its managers in 1986 and then by Volvo in 1988.

Volvo was very fortunate. In its early years in the UK it was selling only a single double-deck bus underframe, the Ailsa, that was being aided by the problems at Leyland, and on the coaching side was selling a single chassis, the B58, primarily to small operators who were not effected by the political changes and who managed their local market sufficiently well to be able to renew and upgrade their fleets.

By the time that B10M and its successors came along the industry was recovering, along with the economy, and there was an urgent need for fleet renewal and expansion as household disposable income rose and leisure travel became more adventurous. By the time Olympian was due for renewal large fleets across the country were also needing to be replaced and the major groups that had emerged were seeking partners in this activity. B10M and B7TL and their successors were to play an important part in this process.

As economically, GB became a richer society, so concern for the disabled members of society rose and especially their access to public transport. This led to the establishment of the Disabled Persons Transport Advisory Committee – DiPTAC. DiPTAC took a fairly pragmatic view of what was needed and drew up a series of requirements that would be implemented over a lengthy time scale – recognising that road and rail vehicles with life spans of up to 20 years – even more in the rail industry – could not be altered overnight.

The major impact of DiPTAC on the bus manufacturing industry was to push it more rapidly than might otherwise have been the case to low-floor, easy-access vehicle designs. Volvo was not exempt from this pressure and the legislative requirements that went with it, especially as, by the 1990s, it had become a major player in the UK and Irish bus market. It was not an easy transition for Volvo.

Not only Westminster has an impact on the domestic market. Transport for London sets the specification for all the buses operated in London and Volvo's B7TL double-deck chassis fell foul of TfL regulations. In 2006 TfL determined that the B7TL was too noisy and identified the air cooling fan system as being the culprit. Although B7TL satisfied all European regulations for noise TfL demanded a lower noise level. As a consequence Volvo had to retrofit a solution to over 400 buses to reduce cooling fan noise. It also meant that no new B7TL were authorised for use in London – leading to the introduction of the B9TL chassis.

DiPTAC brought low-floor buses into prominence. This B6BLE/Wright, above left, although liveried for London General, was, in fact, a Volvo demonstration vehicle. (DC)

The innovative B10L, left, was an early contender to satisfy low-floor requirements. It was, however, complex and expensive and enjoyed only a limited success in the UK and Irish markets. The demonstrator is seen here in Sheffield. (STA)

The B7TL (above) fell foul of noise regulations specific only to London and had to receive modifications. B9TL (lower) satisfied even London regulations. (TQ both)

(b) – Europe

From Europe came both help and hindrance for Volvo in the UK. The establishment of the Common Market in 1957 had wide implications for those outside its framework. The Common Market would reduce internal tariffs but have a common external tariff. Eventually Britain joined the Common Market, but Sweden elected to stay outside this framework. Europe was an important market for Volvo and it could not afford to be 'frozen out' by a tariff wall. The idea, therefore, of producing vehicles in Britain – a state inside the tariff wall – was very attractive and contributed substantially to the decision by Volvo to both produce vehicles at Irvine and, later, to purchase Leyland with its facility at Workington.

Brussels was as prone to interfere with the bus industry as Westminster. The quality of the environment, including air quality in cities, became a concern of the EU. The emissions from diesel engines were perceived to be especially harmful and so Brussels began to establish minimum standards of exhaust emissions from diesel engines. At first, these were not especially onerous to meet, but as progress at approximately 5 year intervals went from Euro 1 in 1993 in to Euro 2 and on to Euro 5 and Euro 6 the design of diesel engines had to be radically, and expensively, rethought. At a time when a major concern of operators is with fuel consumption it is strange that the politicians in Brussels were uncaring about this element. All of Volvo's offerings to the market after 1993 complied fully with the European requirements. Volvo followed the path of placing additives into fuel – eg Ad Blu – to achieve the requirements of Euro 4 and Euro 5, but Euro 6 has required some radical redesign of diesel engines.

An offshoot of this desire for clean air was the hybrid bus, the Volvo B5LH double-deck and 7900 single-deck – basically using a small(ish) diesel engine to drive an electric transmission. Ironically the principles behind the hybrid bus are those of the very early Tilling-Stevens petrol-electric buses over 100 years ago! Volvo had an early attempt at hybrid technology with the Cumulo Citybus in London – a vehicle ahead of its time – and it is, perhaps, no accident that the Volvo hybrid double-decker, B5LH, is regarded as the most reliable of the hybrid designs.

Euro 1 = 1993	Euro 2 = 1996
Euro 3 = 2001	Euro 4 = 2006
Euro 5 = 2009	Euro 6 = 2014

Externally this Wright-bodied B5LH is virtually indistinguishable from its diesel counterpart – Travel for London being content with a small 'hybrid' logo. The technology, however, is rather more complex, requiring new technician skills and maintenance regimes. (TQ)

Volvo's single-deck hybrid bus, the 9700, is, however, very distinctive. Lothian Transport is the largest user of this marque, operating 50 examples, with a further 25 vehicles expected. (BE)

Chapter 2
Volvo Coaches From the B58 to the B11R

Wilson at Stainforth (t/a Premier) was amongst the very earliest operators of the B58, one being seen above with a Plaxton body. This represented the height of sophistication when the vehicle was delivered new in February of 1973. (MB)

The contrast with the Plaxton Elitei-bodied B11R delivered to Stagecoach for its Megabus operation is vast. This vehicle has air conditioning, at-seat entertainment, a galley, reclining seats, wi-fi and many other passenger-friendly attachments. Plaxton have been the dominant supplier of coach bodies throughout the period in which Volvo has been in the UK and Irish markets. (PL)

21

B58 Coach Chassis

'In the beginning was BUS 653K…' – the forerunner to many thousands of Volvo coach chassis sold for use in the British Isles. It was extensively used as a demonstrator – here with Grey-Green. It passed to Aston's at Kempsey who extended the chassis and rebodied it with a Van Hool body. After over 40 years service it has only recently been withdrawn from daily use. (MB)

This iconic chassis came to dominate the UK quality operator market for almost 10 years and transformed coach travel for passengers and operators alike. Not all of which, of course, can be attributed to Volvo – the growth of the motorway network, growing wealth in the population leading to a demand for higher standards, and the political manipulation of the motor industry leading to an almost total neglect of Leyland Bus and Truck all played their part. But the Volvo B58 was the 'right chassis, in the right place, at the right time' and Volvo were fortunate in having a team in the UK, led from 1978 onwards by Sandy Glennie, that was entrepreneurial, innovative and very, very customer focussed – qualities that were unevenly distributed and often sadly lacking in the UK manufacturing industry.

The first B58 chassis was imported to the UK in about 1970, but was not bodied until 1972 when Alexanders built a Y-type express body. BUS 653K, as this vehicle became, was used by Ailsa as a demonstrator and was seen throughout the UK in this role. It was then sold and used by a variety of independent operators. By 1983 it was with Astons at Kempsey, near Worcester, who took the body off, lengthened the chassis at Evesham Technical College, and then sent the refurbished chassis to Van Hool for rebodying. The resulting vehicle has continued to 'earn its keep' and is now with Village Green Bus Co in Herefordshire where, until very recently, it was used on a daily basis for school transport. This vehicle still has its original engine and gearbox – a remarkable tribute to its initial sturdy construction.

The initial target for B58 was bus companies, especially within the SBG, rather than coach operators. This was in line with Ailsa Bus' thrust with the Ailsa double-deck underframe. Leyland, as already suggested, had seen the potential threat from the B58 and 'warned off' Plaxton and Duple from bodying the chassis. The Yeates dealership in Loughborough, with no links to Leyland, but very strong links to both Duple and Plaxton which they sold on Bedford and Ford chassis, saw an opportunity to move into heavyweight vehicles. Yeates, in turn, leant on Plaxton and Duple – to greater effect than Leyland – and for the 1973 season both coach-builders products were available on the B58 chassis.

The first Plaxton body was exhibited at the 1972 Commercial Motor Show, destined for Smiths of Upper Heyford in Oxfordshire. (This satisfied customer took subsequent batches with Van Hool coachwork.) The engine for the B58 was the THD engine available at either 210 or 250bhp, the latter a figure far in excess of the power available on Leyland and AEC chassis. 1973 saw over 40 chassis sold, a figure that rose into the 70s in both 1974 and 1975. Orders came, gratifyingly, from both new customers and from repeat business, but a weakness in the design had been identified – the Volvo K19 gearbox. This was described by Doug Jack as 'quirky' – operators, who described it more forcibly, found it difficult to handle as it had been designed for left hand drive chassis – but it took until 1978 to replace this with a ZF option. This delay may be attributed to the decision of Jim McKelvie to retire in 1976 and with him went the initial flair that had driven Ailsa Bus. He was replaced by a 'Volvo man', Stig Arne Olsen, and then in 1977 Sandy Glennie took over the reigns.

Ironically, given the effort that went into wooing the Scottish Bus Group it took until 1975 before the SBG took any B58 chassis when a batch with the striking Alexander M-type body were delivered for us on the Scotland–London routes. No further B58s were purchased as they were regarded as far too sophisticated.

Up to 1978 sales of the B58 had been rather 'back of cigarette packet' matter – based on intuition, the guesses of what dealers thought customers would buy, and the limited experience of the Volvo chassis. Sandy Glennie brought a discipline to this process that led to the analysis of market trends, forthcoming legislation, the economic state of the country and only then to the forecast of sales. This led to reliable delivery of chassis to bodybuilders and to dealers. The, at that time, unique idea of whole life costs was used to persuade operators that the higher cost of B58 chassis was a good investment as it was both more reliable and more durable. This argument was very convincing and sales picked up in 1978 and 1979.

At this point Leyland played into Volvo's hands. In 1978 they announced that they would cease production of both the AEC Reliance and the Leyland Leopard and replace both with a new chassis to be built at Leyland. This, of course, implied that fewer dealers would be required and a number of dealers moved their allegiance to Volvo – this included Stanley Hughes and Kirkby who were able to influence Wallace Arnold and Smiths Happiways respectively to add B58s to their vehicle intake. Not surprisingly in the climate of the time, Leyland were very late producing details of the new chassis and operators were left with the option of purchasing soon-to-be obsolete Leyland or AECs, or Volvo's B58.

By 1979 the UK operation of Volvo was the leading single-deck coach market in the Volvo empire having registered over 310 sales for the B58. This represented over 40% of the UK and Ireland market for heavy coaches – a dramatic rise from 2.5% only 6 years earlier. In order to achieve this the B58 chassis had been updated with an option of air-over-leaf suspension and the K19 gearbox had been destined to history. Because of the very low centre of gravity of the B58 it was possible for coachbuilders to build higher floor coaches, culminating in the Plaxton Viewmaster on a B58 chassis – the first UK-built coach to make any real attempt to challenge the continental integral coachbuilders such as Setra. This ability to build a premium body on the B58, combined with the excellent service and support network that Volvo had in place in Europe, meant that any operator expecting to have work that took his or her vehicles across the Channel had little real option. As Leyland, Ford and Bedford had virtually no support scheme they either bought a very expensive and somewhat unknown continental marque or a Volvo B58.

Nineteen-eighty promised to be another excellent year for the B58, but it was overshadowed by the development in Sweden of the B10M as a replacement. Volvo Bus (Great Britain) – as it had become in the summer of 1979 – decided to run the two chassis in parallel for 1980 with B10M marketed at a premium. They,

Hills at Tredegar were early converts to the B58. Having acquired this Plaxton-bodied example with the business of Davies in the same town, Hills subsequently purchased new vehicles. (MB)

Aston's at Kempsey purchased a number of part-used B58s. This Plaxton-bodied machine, below, began life with Spanner and Walker at St. Albans before moving north to Worcestershire. (DC)

Looking every inch the 'executive vehicle' in its distinctive livery, this immaculate Plaxton Viewmaster-bodied B58 of Parks of Hamilton awaits its returning passengers. This chassis-body combination was the first real attempt in the UK to challenge the continental integral coaches. The Volvo B58-Viewmaster was a powerful machine, with ample luggage space and the ability to carry heavy, luxury fittings. (MB)

therefore, exhibited a B58 at the Scottish Show in autumn of 1979 – a 12-metre chassis with air-over-leaf suspension and the trusty ZF gearbox – and ordered 300 B58 chassis at a very favourable price to run out production at Boras and for delivery on the UK and Ireland over 1980 and into 1981. During that period, in April 1981, the 1,000th B58 chassis was delivered to a UK operator. In this period, too, a newly formed company took delivery of B58s – Stagecoach. In Stagecoach hands they amassed very high mileages, often travelling from Aberdeen to London and back in a 24 hour period. A relationship that has endured over 30 years had begun.

Numerically, the last chassis delivered was 16774 to Astons at Kempsey in March 1982. (Astons also, of course, by then owned the first B58, chassis 326, the ex-demonstrator BUS 653K). The last B58s to enter service were a batch for Smiths at Wigan a month later. A total of almost 1,300 B58 chassis had been delivered to the UK and Irish market and had a lasting impact on the British coaching scene.

As the market grew more discerning, so some customers wished to move away from the duopoly of Plaxton and Duple. Van Hool were first on the scene, offering their Spanish-built body through the Moseley dealership. Moseley had established a separate company to import Caetano bodies from Portugal, initially on Bedford chassis, but quickly added Volvo to the chassis options. This became a very successful combination. Moseley also imported Unicar bodies with rather less success, only 16 having Volvo chassis. A somewhat maverick John de Costa also had several B58 chassis bodied by Irizar with their unusual 'Urko' one-and-a-half-deck body.

A number of B58 chassis came to Britain but were destined for other markets. In 1974 Duple had decided that it would enter the export market. In conjunction with Moseley, the dealer, and Volvo it produced the 'Goldliner' body, a UK specification body modified to meet Swedish regulations and conditions. Only 3 vehicles went to Sweden, but a larger batch went to Australia. The latter looked like a promising venture until the Australian trade unions became involved and import duties on completed vehicles mysteriously rose very sharply indeed! Equally interestingly, a small number of used chassis were imported to the UK and rebodied by Willowbrook before being re-exported to Denmark.

Buses are not usually associated with the B58 chassis. However, Volvo were keen to test the bus market and a small number of chassis received bus bodies. Their initial choice of partner seems strange in retrospect. Wadham Stringer were associated with welfare vehicles and had no customer base amongst bus operators. Nonetheless, they built a single body that was used by Volvo as a demonstrator and then sold to the A1 co-operative without generating any other business. More promising was the decision by Duple to offer their bus body on the B58 chassis which resulted in a small number of sales to independent operators.

Whippet took two 63-seat examples, the A1 co-operative took examples along with Hutchisons at Overtown and Graham at Paisley who took several 53-seat examples. A single Plaxton Derwent bus body went to Wright at Wrexham. These sales were never going to 'set the heather alight' but were an interesting pointer to a market that would be very important for the B10M.

The flat frame of the B58 also appealed to a totally different market – horse-boxes. At least 6 horse-boxes were constructed on B58 chassis. The most high profile was that belonging to Sir Hugh Fraser of House of Fraser fame – HOF 1. This was built by Jennings but Oakley and Lambourn also built on the chassis. Three chassis were bodied by Van Plan as pantechnicons, one being used for the transport of antiques from Ireland and one, owned by Volvo for a short period, was kitted out as a hospitality vehicle. Perhaps the most unusual body on a B58 was what became the 'Hercmobile' – an extensively modified Van Hool body that provided the living accommodation for Hercules the Bear as he toured the UK visiting fairs, fêtes etc; eventually both Hercules and his accommodation were shipped to the USA.

By 1982 the B58 had established Volvo as the dominant player in the UK coach market. The Volvo reputation for support and service had established new standards that others found hard to emulate, let alone surpass. After 1978 Sandy Glennie also brought rigorous management techniques to bus and coach sales. The somewhat lackadaisical days of building bodies without chassis and holding chassis for long periods awaiting slots at the bodybuilders had gone for ever, and B58 was the tool that enabled this transition to be made.

The B58 chassis appealed to operators of all sizes. Wright's at Wrexham – a small but ambitious operator – took this well specified Plaxton Supreme-bodied-example. The rather bleak winter view is at the operating centre at Pen-y-Cae.

Wallace Arnold was at the other end of the scale, a large operator who, at that time, controlled the Evan Evans brand. This example, another Plaxton Supreme-bodied vehicle, stands, appropriately, outside the Grand Hotel.

Trathen's at Yelverton were an aggressive rapidly growing operator who had captured much of the 'sun run' traffic to the South of France. They needed reliable vehicles with a European support system. This Duple-bodied vehicle, with Globus Gateway slipboards, delivered in March 1979, is captured on a rally at Chesil Beach. (DC all)

Caetano, from Portugal, had also entered the market by 1979. Trathen's not only operated on the 'sun run' to France, but also contracted to offer tours to incoming tourists. Caetano were judged to be sufficiently luxurious to work the prestigious Townsend Thoresen contract. These robust vehicles were to carry several contract liveries before leaving Trathens service.

For almost six years bodybuilding on B58 was virtually dominated by Plaxton and Duple – the former taking the lion's share. By 1977, however, operators were demanding more 'exotic' products and more variety. Van Hool offered the predecessor of the Alizee, which brought it to the British market for the first time. The early models, such as this example operating for Redby of Sunderland, were built in Spain.

Jonckheere had been the first coachbuilder to break the Plaxton/Duple duopoly, with a neat, well-finished and conservative but stylish design. Wright/Buddens at Woodfalls in Hampshire took a batch of the Bermuda design in 1981, one of which is depicted below on UK tour work. (DC all)

A less successful entrant to the UK market was Unicar, another Spanish coachbuilder. Although stylish, the build quality was poor and only a small number of B58 chassis carried this bodywork – repeat orders failed to materialise. Bowens were a well-established Birmingham operator and this photograph, taken in high summer, shows their only Unicar-bodied B58. (DC)

Even more exotic, and equally rare, was the Irizar `Urko' bodywork with a 'semi-half-deck' body style. Madison Travel used this example as the Wolverhampton Wanderers Team Coach when it was new. These strongly built coaches had a long life and at least one is now in preservation. (DC)

Rare, but in a rather different way, is this 1980 delivered Plaxton-bodied B58, with Glenton Tours unique central entrance. This very up-market operator specialised in incoming wealthy Australian tourists. A savage downturn in the Australian economy led to the demise of this characterful operator. (MB)

27

The striking Alexander 'M' type body sat well on the B58. The underfloor engine made it slightly higher than the Bristol RE stablemate, both pictured at Kilmarnock. The later Citylink livery seen below was far less striking than the original 'Scottish' scheme but enabled these vehicles to be used on internal Scottish services as well as the London service for which they were originally purchased. (JS)

When withdrawn by Western a number of these coaches found further service with independent operators wishing to provide high levels of comfort. Graham's at Paisley used them to good effect on the 'Linwood Clipper' express service from Glasgow to Linwood. (MB)

The trapezoid windows designed for the Scottish overnight services were never very popular. A unique example was a Duple Dominant III to express specification for The Eden services in Bishop Auckland. (MB)

28

By 1980 the B58 had become the dominant heavyweight chassis in the UK and formed the base for nearly all Executive coaches. This example for Barry Cooper at Stockton Heath very clearly reflects the owner's view that with his Plaxton Viewmaster-bodied B58 he has bought 'the best'. (MB)

A significant early sale of a B58 was to a small, upstart operator who had begun to create a niche market with a long distance express service from Aberdeen to London, used primarily by oil workers. Coaches stopped at Walnut Grove, near Perth, to upload sandwiches and coffee prepared by the operator's mother. And so Stagecoach was born! The early 'Stagecoach stripes' are seen in a rather damp Glasgow. (RC)

Another operator to benefit from the oil boom in Scotland in the early 1980s was Newton at Dingwall. Newton provided transport from a very wide area to the oil rig construction facility at Nigg Bay. He also provided express services to Lowland Scotland, chiefly Glasgow, using a fleet of B58s bodied by both Plaxton and Duple. Two Plaxton-bodied examples sit in the evening sun at Dingwall. (RC)

Very much a one off! The 'Hercmobile' was home both to Hercules the performing bear and his trainer. The much modified interior of the Van Hool body is not apparent in this view taken in Milngavie at Carnival time in 1984. Thirty years later the animal rights organisations would ensure that such a vehicle was never built. (RC)

29

More conventional Van Hool bodies were delivered to Hutchisons at Overtown, south of Glasgow. These vehicles were operated on express services into Glasgow as well as on private hire and incoming tours. It is interesting that 'Executive' has been replaced by 'Pullman' to denote the peak of luxury. (RC)

In the early period of de-regulated express services the appropriately named Flights Travel of Birmingham developed a network of services linking the major English airports. The 'Flightlink' network used high specification coaches to operate inter-airport as well as more conventional services to and from airports. This Plaxton Viewmaster-bodied B58 is on the approaches to Spaghetti Junction on the M5. (DC)

Also purchased for airport work was this Duple-bodied B58 of London Country's Green Line operation. Volvo devoted much, rather fruitless, energy into gaining sales from the NBC and related companies and this small order marked something of a breakthrough. Although being used on a private hire, the luggage racking is clearly visible on the front offside of the bodywork. (DC)

Volvo's first single-deck bus for the British market. This Duple-bodied B58 was a 'toe in the water' to see whether operators would purchase a premium chassis for bus work. The answer was 'Yes' – there were a few discriminating operators who were confident enough to buy a service bus with a 15 year design life. Longstaff at Mirfield was an established Volvo coach operator so had full knowledge of the chassis. The bus lasted in service appreciably longer than its design life! (DC)

Whippet, a long-standing Cambridgeshire operator, also tried the new combination, but attempted to offset the high cost of the new bus by having 3+2 seating giving 70 seats in total – as many as a contemporary double-deck vehicle but in a much more flexible form. Like Longstaff's vehicle, this ran in service for many, many years. (MB)

Strangely, Volvo turned to Wadham-Stringer to body its B58 bus demonstrator, with an unusual agreement whereby Wadham-Stringer continued to own the body and Volvo the chassis. The well-specified vehicle, finished to dual-purpose standards, was sold to A1 Services at Ardrossan and so passed the gates of the Volvo Irvine factory with great regularity. (RC)

31

A single example of the B58 bus was bodied by Plaxton with its neat 'Bustler' body. This was purchased by the enterprising independent Wright's of Wrexham and used on their local services around that town, often competing with Crosville. In later life this vehicle became a mobile fish and chip shop. An ignominious end for an interesting vehicle. (MB)

Forty years old and still going strong! The original B58 eventually passed to Aston's at Kempsey near Worcester. There, the chassis was lengthened to 12 metres and rebodied by Van Hool. In 2014 it was still 'earning its keep' in the hands of the Village Motor Services in Herefordshire. It does, apparently, still have the original engine and gearbox though the unique white steering wheel was replaced when it was rebodied. A tribute to the quality of the Volvo engineering. (RC)

B10M Coach Chassis

B58 had established Volvo in the British market. B10M consolidated this position and enabled Volvo to go forward into the 1980s with a fresh product. Volvo announced the B10M at the 1980 Geneva Motor Show in January.

The main difference between the two chassis was that the B10M had a jig welded chassis frame – at that time very innovative – rather than the bolted frame of the B58, and air suspension was standard on the B10M. The engine for the B10M was still the THD 100 engine, but newly modified to be both more powerful and more fuel efficient. The new engine allowed Volvo to meet the German Tempo 100 rules that required minimum power to weight ratios. This was an important consideration in the UK where increasing numbers of operators were taking coaches to the European mainland. The air suspension also allowed high floor bodies to be built on the chassis, a major consideration for tour operators who dealt with incoming Japanese and American tourists who, almost invariably, carried vast amounts of luggage.

It is worthwhile recalling that at the time of the B10M launch in to the UK Volvo was the only major importer of coach chassis. Mercedes had tried and withdrawn. MAN had still to bring the SR280 integral to the UK. DAF and Scania were still only 'putting a toe in the water'. Bova was the only serious importer, using the Moseley dealership – who also handled Volvo with Van Hool bodies. Leyland was still reliant upon the Leopard with the AEC Reliance also in their stable. Sales of Bedford and Ford lightweight chassis were declining sharply.

The B10M became iconic, and none more so than when teamed with a Plaxton body. Although the B10M was used for all manner of purposes it is, perhaps, as a touring coach with one of the major groups that it will remain in people's memories. This Plaxton-bodied example with Wallace Arnold awaits its returning passengers at Glenshee. (KM)

B10M was initially available with Duple, Plaxton, Jonckheere, Van Hool and Caetano bodywork – an impressive range of choice for operators and by the middle of 1981 all five coachbuilders had delivered vehicles to UK operators. A more exotic choice of bodywork for delivery in 1982 was selected by Trathens, in the shape of the Padane ZX. These fully air-conditioned, very high specification coaches were used almost exclusively on work for Townsend Thoresen cruise line. No other operator followed the Trathen example. Ensign, better known for selling second-hand vehicles, had acted as Padane's agent for this sale and clearly thought there was a niche market for coach sales alongside their more traditional business. However, recognising that Padane was an extremely expensive option, they tied up with Berkhof, a relatively new company operating in the Netherlands.

Having demonstrated an early example to Western SMT, that operator quickly ordered a batch of B10M with Duple bodywork for the arduous Scotland-London services. Alexanders, who had produced the American Greyhound-like, M-type coachwork for the SBG, and which had been fitted to a batch of B58 chassis, had declined this order and Duple produced a very attractive variation of the Dominant with trapezoid windows that mimicked the Alexander M-type. This window variation was also taken by a few other operators and by Parks of Hamilton in a large order for high-floor coaches delivered in 1982 and named by Duple the Goldliner.

Duple, at that time, were being quite innovative and took on another venture with Volvo and Parks of Hamilton to produce an articulated coach, primarily for Glasgow-London operation, using the motorway network to full advantage. This was little problem for Volvo who produced articulated coaches for other markets. Three shortened chassis were delivered to Blackpool, along with articulation kit, but, even as the chassis were being prepared for bodying, the Ministry of Transport issued an edict banning coaches from the outside lane of motorways. Parks decided that this would lead to extended journey times and the project was abandoned. The chassis were extended and bodied as 'normal' vehicles.

It was noticeable that Volvo had failed to penetrate the National Bus Company market. This was hardly surprising, given the link of NBC to Leyland, but even NBC had to recognise that if they were to enter into contracts taking them into Europe they had to have a better support system than that provided by Leyland. The breakthrough came in 1984 when the imaginatively titled National Travel East won a major contract with Club 18-30 and also with Intasun, both of which required extensive operation in the European mainland. NT(E) ordered no less than 26 B10Ms with Jonckheere coachwork, six of which were double-deck vehicles and were designed with ski-boxes attached to the rear.

With deregulation of express services a number of operators began commuter services into London, most notably The Kings Ferry who purchased a major fleet of Berkhof-bodied B10Ms. Other operators initiated express services to challenge the SBG and NBC domination of this sector. In Scotland, where this challenge was especially fierce, Allanders at Milngavie, Newtons at Dingwall and Parks of Hamilton all began long distance operations. In England, Trathens were aggressive players. All used the B10M.

Coach touring was also becoming more concentrated. Smiths at Wigan and Shearings had become a group, and then taken over Salopia. Wallace Arnold continued to flourish and expand. The Excelsior Group also flourished. In the absence of a reliable and modern competitor they all used Volvo B10M chassis with a variety of coachwork. Smiths amassed the largest Volvo fleet in the country by 1984 when it took 32 examples, bringing its fleet of Volvos to 145. In Scotland, Parks had just under 100 Volvos, most of them under 4 years old.

Coachbuilders were not slow to wish to body B10M. Yeates, the dealer, took on LAG for 1985. Douglas Telfer decided that he wished to be independent and so left the security of a post at Volvo, and established Tramontana at Motherwell in Scotland as both an operator and dealer, working with Irizar who at that time produced the Pyrenean body. Not to be outdone by Caetano, who were selling well on the B10M chassis, fellow Portuguese body-builder Camo built an example of its product for the UK market – it was destined to remain unique. The same fate befell a very high specification coach built on a B10MT chassis by Ajokki. Van Rooijen also bodied a single example for the UK for 1984 but had problems with their agents and no further example followed. Wrights also bodied a single example with their Contour body that had previously been built in small numbers on Bedford Y-type chassis. The most successful incursion came from Eastern Europe when Kirkby, the dealer, teamed up with Ikarus to

A useful way of gaining publicity for a new vehicle was to enter a high specification example in the Brighton Coach Rally. Winning gave prestige not only to operator, but also to the chassis and bodybuilder. PAY 2W of Clarke's of Loughborough has won Coach of the Year award. A useful boost to the new chassis. (DC)

An early purchaser of the B10M chassis was Wings at Sleaford. This example has a Plaxton Elite IV body that was unusual in having flat side glass windows. It was not a popular option. Worthy of note is the 'bottom step' carefully painted into Wings livery. This was a necessary accessory in the days before 'kneeling' suspension. (DC)

bring their Blue Danube body to the UK for 1986. The great bulk of the B10M chassis, however, were bodied by Plaxton, Duple, Jonckheere, Van Hool and Caetano, with Berkhof occupying a significant minority slot.

By the end of 1985 – a year in which Volvo sold almost 300 chassis in the UK – Volvo determined to upgrade the B10M to keep it abreast of modern engine technology and to upgrade many of the auxiliary features. The Mk II B10M had a more efficient TDH101 engine with power rating available up to 310bhp, recognising the additional power necessary to sustain the road performance of the chassis and also recognising the need for power to drive all manner of features such as air conditioning by then regarded as standard. The chassis was also made more driver-friendly with a new instrument panel and adjustable steering column.

1985 also saw the Transport Act passed through Parliament in London. The result was to decimate the bus and coach market. Leyland was especially hard hit as its major customer was the National Bus Company which was to be broken into small subsidiaries and then sold. This weakening of Leyland was to prove fatal. But Volvo, having failed to gain entry to the NBC market, was relatively unscathed by this development. The holiday groups and the smaller operators remained 'in the market' – Wallace Arnold, for example, took 32 chassis in 1986. The consequence of this was that Volvo's market share rose sharply – to over 40% – though in a smaller market.

Despite the depressed market Volvo continued to sell more chassis each year. In 1989 the chassis was again upgraded and became the Mk III. These developments were driven more by the requirements of European operators than British ones, but nonetheless were incorporated into chassis built for the UK and Ireland. A whole range of improvements were made to the specification. The THD engine was further developed to become the THD102 and give an output of either 260bhp or 340bhp in UK applications. Externally the most obvious change was to see two radiators on the nearside of the vehicle – one a classic radiator and the other for the intercooler. Emission levels were reduced again, and came well within EEC regulations. For the driver the major innovation was the Volvo Easy Shift gearbox and control – the latter being a miniature gearstick mounted on the seat frame and so moving with the driving position. The Volvo gearbox was the first to be offered after the problems with the K19 box on early B58 chassis. The problems were not repeated!

Demonstrating the flexibility of the B10M platform, British Caledonian Airways took delivery of four 18m articulated vehicles in 1990 for use airside at Gatwick airport. These vehicles had a capacity for 140 passengers. Two further Van Hool-bodied vehicles were to follow in 1996 when Ulsterbus took two more conventional examples. Stagecoach, that had inherited many of the Scottish longer distance inter-urban services, wanted to increase capacity without using double-deck vehicles, so they took ten B10MA – 'A' for articulated – chassis with Plaxton bodies and two Jonckheere-bodied examples. They were used not only in Scotland but also to establish new routes in England. Stagecoach also ordered 100 chassis with Plaxton Premier 3200 bodies to an 'InterUrban' specification that enabled them to modernise many routes that fell short of being long-distance yet were more than local services. Delivery of this order took place in 1996 and 1997.

In 1995 a new variant on the coach chassis was produced – the B10M-66. This chassis had the wheelbase extended and the engine and gearbox moved as close to the rear axle as possible in order that a full width luggage locker could be fitted behind the front wheels. This configuration satisfied the market for some of the National Express contractors, such as Durham City Services, and the likes of Flights in Birmingham and Cambridge Coach Services all of whom were engaged in airport services where luggage capacity was at a premium. Only a small number of this variant was sold in the UK.

Rather different from the standard touring coach was Glenton's B10M/Plaxton. This operator pioneered up-market 'executive tours' using very low density seating – only 30 seats in an 11-metre vehicle – and high specification interiors. For a number of years the company, uniquely, specified a central entrance, but eventually cost considerations led them to the more conventional front entrance depicted here. A 'bottom step' has now been integrated into the door mechanism. (MB)

35

In 1994 a further upgrade of the chassis was introduced. A new, more powerful, engine was fitted and many component upgrades were made. Visually the most obvious change was that the radiator was moved from the front of the chassis to the nearside. This model was built for over seven years with the last chassis being bodied by Plaxton for Pulhams at Bourton on the Water.

Following the upgrade to the chassis Volvo successfully broke into the Bus Eireann market with orders for the chassis with Caetano bodies for express services. The last B10Ms to enter service was a large batch of Caetano-bodied vehicles to the Irish operator in July 2001 and some stock vehicles that were delivered into 2002.

The B10M chassis was built at Boras, in Sweden, at a factory opened in 1980 specifically to build bus and coach chassis. B10M was the first chassis to be produced at the new factory. But Boras was not the only place in which B10M was built – it shared that honour with both Irvine and Workington.

By 1985 UK orders for the B10M were rising steadily. This factor combined with the political considerations outlined on page 17 persuaded Volvo to produce the B10M chassis at the Irvine factory. Between August 1995 and the closure of the Irvine plant in early 2000 almost 1400 B10M chassis were produced. The Irvine factory even had its own chassis number sequence beginning at 60001 and ending at 61362. The great majority of Irvine produced chassis were supplied to UK and Irish operators. Deliveries to the UK also continued to be made from Boras.

Once Volvo had taken over Leyland in 1988, there was a major question of how to make the Workington plant profitable. Olympian production was moved to Workington to boost throughput alongside the Lynx, but there was still

The Plaxton Paramount-bodied B10M chassis attracted small operators who ran up-market tours. Rover Tours in Gloucestershire was one of those operators who saw the combination equalling the Volvo/Van Hool pairing. Coupled to a dateless registration this vehicle gave many seasons of top quality work. (RC)

A similar combination attracted Coliseum Coaches of Southampton. Attractive liveries were seen as part of the 'marketing' of the high quality coaching experience. (RC)

36

vast overcapacity. It was, therefore, planned to move some B10M production to Workington in 1990. Doug Jack suggests that there was an initial target of 80 chassis, rising to 200 units over a five year period. The first B10M produced at Workington went to Parks at Hamilton – a sign of confidence in the build quality at Workington. However, depressed trading conditions in the UK meant that the Workington factory was still heavily loss making. The decision to close Workington was taken in December 1991 and production of the B10M in the UK became focussed on Irvine. The Workington factory produced about 300 chassis in total, including a batch of vehicles destined for Iran that required heavy modification of the cooling systems to cope with the Iranian climate.

There were far fewer 'Specials' built on B10M chassis than B58. A single horse box went to Pittington in County Durham to join the Newton stable, followed by two other examples going elsewhere. A rather special vehicle was delivered to the City of Birmingham Symphony Orchestra in 1991. This was a Plaxton 3500 body substantially modified to carry all the orchestra's instruments. It featured a full air conditioning system, and full living accommodation for the driver and, not surprisingly, a high grade security system.

Volvo had 'dipped a toe in the water' for the bus application of the B58. For the B10M, bus application was to become very significant and is dealt with on page 129 in the 'Bus' section of this volume.

Small operators, such as Allanders at Milngavie, pictured here, felt able to confidently undertake European private hire with the B10M. This example, one of many purchased by the company, has unloaded a student group in Luxembourg – but seems anxious to return home. (RC)

Wallace Arnold took many varieties of coachwork on B10M. This example - a Plaxton Paramount III – sits at the outlet shop in Callander awaiting the return of it's passengers. The door is rightly closed to keep the cold winds sweeping down from the snow covered hills at bay. (RC)

37

B10M had little competition in the market for high quality chassis. Unless prepared to pay a very high premium for European integral coaches Leyland's ageing Leopard, and later the Tiger, provided the only alternative. An Epsom Coaches Plaxton-bodied B10M is seen at Heathrow airport, long before the days of low cost airlines. (RC)

Away from the Metropolis smaller operators also appreciated the long-term value of the B10M chassis. This example, with Bibbys at Ingleton in North Yorkshire, was used by the company to enter the Brighton Coach Rally and other publicity events. (RC)

Brian Souter and Stagecoach may imagine that sleeper coaches are novel – they are not. Len Wright Travel, who provided transport for early rock bands, before 'celebrity' overtook them, would move them from gig to gig in their Nightliner coaches, allowing a group to achieve at least a modicum of rest and recuperation! (DC)

38

One of the few 'specials' built on the B10M chassis was this adapted Plaxton Paramount body built for carrying the instruments of the City of Birmingham Symphony Orchestra. By virtue of the value of its cargo it had elaborate security systems, and air conditioning. For an orchestra on tour this was an invaluable vehicle, ensuring that precious instruments arrived at their destination in good condition and under the watchful eye of the driver and support crew. (STA)

The Premier body that Plaxton built on the B10M to supersede the Paramount also found favour with tour operators. An example with Robinsons in North West England sets off from Bolton for the Low Countries. (HP)

The Premier-bodied B10M also found favour with operators who's portfolio included a wide range of customers with very varied demands. This example with the Capitol Group in South Wales operated for all manner of private hires - including the Gwent Diecast Model Club. (DC)

39

Another North West operator who purchased a succession of Plaxton-bodied B10Ms was Battersby Silver Grey, so named after a number of mergers and takeovers. This example has the Premier 320 body – the 320 denoting the height of the vehicle in centimetres. This was a popular choice with small and medium sized operators. (HP)

Shearings were important Volvo customers. This followed the lead of Eric Lomax at Smith Happyway Spencer who had built up a considerable fleet of B58s. When the companies merged the Volvo B10M became the favoured platform. The Plaxton Panther body never quite had the elegance and practicality of its predecessors and followers. (HP)

Wray's of Harrogate were a long-established operator that catered for the up-market needs of conference attendees in that town. This high specification model has an offside exit for European touring in its Plaxton Paramount III 3500 body. The elaborate livery possibly reflects the target market. For smaller groups Wray's was notable for operating one of the few B6 coaches for a while. (DC)

Not all operators could afford to purchase a fleet of brand new vehicles. Woodstone at Kidderminster, an ambitious operation, bought part-used, high specification touring coaches from Wallace Arnold in order to enter the European tours market. Today Woodstones focus on high quality schools work, but are still loyal to the Plaxton/Volvo combination. They are one of the lead customers for the B8R chassis with the new Plaxton Leopard body. (DC)

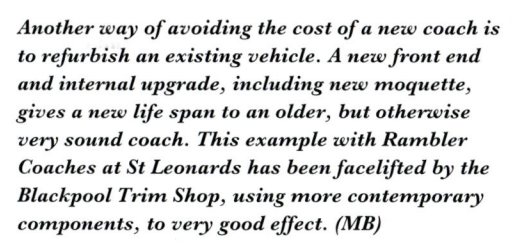

Another way of avoiding the cost of a new coach is to refurbish an existing vehicle. A new front end and internal upgrade, including new moquette, gives a new life span to an older, but otherwise very sound coach. This example with Rambler Coaches at St Leonards has been facelifted by the Blackpool Trim Shop, using more contemporary components, to very good effect. (MB)

Duple were not slow to follow Plaxton in introducing new, high specification coach bodies. This early example of the new Dominant range was one of the very few produced without the roof line continuing to the front windscreen. In the early days of long distance de-regulation this coach passed from Happy Days in Staffordshire to Les Bywater in Rochdale to operate a London service. (DC)

41

When Western SMT ordered B10M chassis for the London service, Alexander's refused the order for coachwork. However, Duple took up the challenge and produced a handsome variation on the Dominant theme, using the trapezoid windows that were deemed necessary for overnight travel. The 'Scottish' livery suited this design well. (JS)

Very few other operators took vehicles to the Western SMT specification, one of the exceptions being Eavesway of Ashton-under-Lyne who took a 36-seat example for high-end charter and football team work. (STA)

Following a fire, one of the Duple-bodied 'London' coaches was rebodied by Western SMT – re-bodying being a long tradition for this Scottish company. (See 'Scottish Rebuilt Buses' John Sinclair, Venture Publications) The Duple Caribbean body is more conventional, but still striking. (MB)

The Duple bodies on the B10M 'London' coaches proved not to be very durable and Western SMT, ever a thrifty company, had them rebodied by East Lancs with a workmanlike 'express' body that was well suited to Scottish inter-urban journeys. Allocated to Ayr Depot, in which town this picture is taken, they operated the Clyde Coaster service north to Greenock. (JS)

West Coast Motors at Campbeltown linked the town with Glasgow on a lengthy service that covered the whole of the Mull of Kintyre. Always impeccably turned out, this B10M with a Duple body waits on the forecourt of the former MacBrayne's depot at Ardrishaig on Loch Fyne. (RC)

When National Travel East gained contracts that took vehicles to Europe the inadequate Leyland support system led the company to acquire Volvo B10Ms. An example with Duple Dominant 3500 body is illustrated here, alongside a lower height example with Smiths Happiways. The location is Callander in Scotland. (RC)

43

Before Citylink became the dominant operator, many long distance services in Scotland were operated by small operators. Skye-Ways at Kyle of Lochalsh operated from Glasgow to Skye. The tough operating conditions required the utmost reliability and good support if 'things went wrong'. A fairly rare Duple Caribbean-bodied B10M of Skye-Ways sits at Glasgow Buchanan Street waiting to take the evening service back to Skye. Skye-Ways also had Monday and Friday services that brought children from remote locations to Kyle where they boarded for the week before going home. (RC)

The Duple Dominant range had been losing market share. Under new management, determined to reverse this loss, Duple produced the low-floor 'Laser' design that was intended to cut fuel consumption by being more aerodynamic. Southern Coaches at Barrhead near Glasgow took an early example, seen here awaiting an incoming ferry at Dunoon. (RC)

Smith's of Murton on Tees-side also took an example of this combination. It is seen here on National Express duty climbing away from the Birmingham Digbeth Coach Station bound for home territory in Sunderland. Operators were dismayed to find that only twelve months after launching these models Duple replaced them, thereby quickly lowering the value of their investment. This move undermined confidence in Duple and contributed to the ultimate demise of the company. (DC)

44

The short-lived Duple Caribbean found relatively few customers. Amongst them was Bere Regis and District who used their example for tour work. Bere Regis struggled to serve a largely rural area with a large but elderly fleet and was one of the earlier independents to find costs rising much faster than revenue, and thus being forced into liquidation. (DC)

Few operators used the B10M-based Caribbean body for high specification coaches. An exception to this was Michael's at Carshalton. The range of extras and the elaborate livery distinguish this Top Executive coach from lesser vehicles. Higher specifications by customers was always welcome by coachbuilders as such vehicles were appreciably more profitable than the standard product. (DC)

Competition amongst the coachbuilders had increased and Jonckheere established itself as the builder of a stylish, robust and well-finished product. Club Cantabrica Holidays at St Albans became a consistent user of the Jonckheere product. (DC)

45

With contracts to operate deep into Europe, National Travel East turned not only to Volvo chassis but also to a European bodybuilder to give security of support. They selected Jonckheere. An example is seen in Club 18-30 livery destined for overnight travel across Europe to holiday destinations in Italy, Greece and Spain. (DC)

Jonckheere, like Van Hool, developed their designs over a number of years so that operators were not left with a clearly dated 'last year's model' and the consequent high depreciation costs. Delivered seven years after the Club 18-30 example above this delivery to Scancoaches, seen at Heathrow on incoming tour work, is clearly from the same design stable but subtly updated. (RC)

The design has been further developed in this Stagecoach example in service on the Cumbrian Connection and loading in Keswick. The coach is operated by Cumberland Motor Services. This was one of a batch of Jonckheere-bodied B10Ms placed in service by Stagecoach on a wide range of inter-urban duties. Not a 'Stagecoach Stripe' to be seen. (HP)

The market in Ireland has always been distinctive and Irish operators have always had a good 'eye for a bargain' – essential in a largely rural country. Healy in Galway acquired this Jonckheere-bodied B10M in 2010, some 14 years after it was built, expecting it to serve as a front line coach. (MB)

The Caetano body developed a good reputation as a sturdy 'maid of all work' product when allied to the B10M chassis. This example with the small fleet of Sean Maher began life as with JJ Kavanagh at Urlingford who used it for incoming tourists. It passed through several hands before reaching the depicted operator. (MB)

Caetano established their reputation with the Algarve body, illustrated here on a B10M of Bebb, Lantwit Fardre in South Wales, later to become a front line National Express contractor. (DC)

In common with other coachbuilders, Caetano had to respond to the need for increased luggage space. The result was an elegant, high-floor version of their Algarve body. Bullocks at Cheadle near Manchester used this vehicle to cater for incoming tourists with their proverbial amounts of luggage. (JAS)

For many operators the Volvo/Van Hool combination was the epitomisation of high class, high quality coaching. Van Hool's Alizee body was a well built, well finished product that matched the qualities of the B10M chassis. Sworder, at Walkern, clearly found this the ideal combination for their Super Executive Coach. (DC)

Skills at Nottingham were prodigious Volvo B10M purchasers, with coachwork by a variety of builders. This Van Hool example has colour flashes in a style that was popular at the time. (DC)

48

By the time this Van Hool-bodied B10M entered service Smiths Happiway Spencer had given way to Smiths Shearings – though they still claimed to be 'Kings of the Road'. B481 UNB is on tour to Inverness and Ullapool – which may explain the rain! (DC)

The Volvo B10M Van Hool combination was very versatile. Newton's at Dingwall took a batch for their express services from the Highlands to the Central Belt of Scotland, challenging Citylink. The challenge led to a buyout by Citylink. This example is seen shortly after the takeover with Highland Omnibuses fleet number and the inevitable paper stickers. (MB)

Cotters Coach Line also challenged the Scottish Bus Group with a premium service from Glasgow and Edinburgh to London, offering a 1st class 'lounge' as well as standard seating. These coaches made a return journey to London every day, quickly amassing very high mileages and thereby justifying the expenditure on premium vehicles. Cotters also acted as Volvo and Van Hool agents for a while. (RC)

49

Cyril Kenzie, a long time Volvo purchaser, took this Van Hool-bodied example in 1987. It is seen on tour, returning to Inveraray on the shores of Loch Fyne, having explored the Mull of Kintyre. (RC)

The split windscreen and subtle livery variations make this Van Hool-bodied B10M of Allander Travel at Milngavie, near Glasgow, look very different from Kenzies coach, above. (RC)

Pictured at Glasgow's Buchanan Street Bus Station, the high-floor Van Hool Alizee of Skye-Ways awaits the afternoon departure to Skye. Before being finally absorbed by Citylink the service was marketed by that company, giving through ticketing. In consequence the route received a Citylink Route Number, just visible on the slip board in the windscreen. (RC)

50

After service with Cotters on their London route OFA 990 passed to Morrison's at Whiteness for further 'express' use in a physically more hostile environment. 'The Orkney Bus' would take passengers from Inverness – where it is pictured – to John O'Groats for the passenger ferry to Burwick on Orkney, timetabled as a day trip to Kirkwall; not Glasgow to London but still well over 100 miles! (JS)

Operated by Halcrow of Cunningsborough in the Shetland Island is this B10M rebodied by Macedonian Metal Industries – one of a small number so treated by Dunn-Line in Nottingham. The MMI bodies were described by some as 'cheap and nasty' and most did not last very long. This example was a remarkable exception, and lasted well into 2013 in an atmosphere that was salt laden and hostile to anything metal. (MB)

Not something to be found in the United Kingdom. In Ireland, however, dealership arrangements were different! This Marcopolo-bodied B10M was imported to Ireland from the Netherlands in 2005 and was acquired twelve months later by McDonagh, operating from Renmore in County Galway. (MB)

Ensign at Purfleet, a well known dealer in used buses and coaches, offered a B10M chassis bodied by the small Dutch coachbuilder, Berkhof, to the market. Trathen's purchased several examples. Liveried for Contiki Travel, this early example of Berkhof coachwork is pictured on a UK tour at Kyle of Lochalsh. (KM)

Trathens also took a small batch of Italian-built Padane-bodied B10Ms primarily for very high quality incoming Townsend Thoresen cruise passengers, but also for their own holiday programme. They were slightly exotic and far too expensive for the British market. Trathens B10Ms were the only Padane bodies built for the UK on Volvo chassis. (DC)

Another manufacturer eager to tap into the British market was the Spanish builder, Irizar. The Pyrenean was a sturdy body but having sold only 12 examples of the model it was seven years before Irizar re-entered the British market. This example is seen at the Scottish Motor Show. (DC)

A unique vehicle was this Wright Contour-bodied B10M delivered new to Liddell of Auchinleck in Ayrshire and operated by him for many years. It had taken Wrights so long to build the body that the chassis had to be upgraded before delivery to Liddell – it was almost four years 'out of sequence'. Another of those interesting 'might have beens'! (RC)

A more determined effort to enter the British market was made by Ikarus, through the Kirkby dealership, where batches of 30 were imported from Hungary. Although stylish and cost effective, the build quality was poor and water ingress a problem, several needing to be rebodied. This example shows the clean styling that made them initially attractive. (MB)

The Van Hool-bodied airside coaches operated by British Caledonian at Gatwick were unique in having both near and offside doors – in profusion. These vehicles were unregistered as they did not run on public roads and were taken to and from maintenance facilities on trade plates. (STA)

53

B9M Coach Chassis

The success of the B10M chassis in 12m configuration led to a demand from a small group of operators for a shorter chassis that would enable a 9m vehicle to be built that would suit smaller parties, or which would give reliable operation for the intensive, virtually 24 hour, operations to car parks and hotels around Heathrow airport. The 'small coach' market was not large but it tended to be high profile.

Volvo responded positively to this request by producing the B10M-48, otherwise known as the B9M. It was relatively easy to engineer this shorter framed B10M which was fitted with all the features of the B10M but with the only engine option being the THD101 engine, rated at 242bhp.

Coachwork on this chassis was dominated by Plaxton but Van Hool also offered a product, both of which were very neat in appearance. Plaxton also bodied a number of these chassis with the Bustler bus body for use by Ralph's Coaches at Langley near Heathrow. A few of the bus-bodied version found a use after life at Heathrow in start-up operations encouraged by de-regulation.

Sales of the B10M-48 were never spectacular – it was a very specialised market – but as the additional cost of producing this variation of the chassis was minimal the model continued to sell in small packages throughout the 1990s.

B9M was notable as being the only chassis actually operated by Volvo. A Van Hool-bodied example became Volvo Bus Ltd's sole vehicle in 1994.

The largest concentration of B10M-48s was to be found around Heathrow Airport. The chassis was a popular one for the almost 24 hour operation of hotel shuttles around the airport. Both the neat Plaxton Bustler bus body and the Paramount coach body were to be found in these duties. The dominant operator at that time was Ralph's Coaches based at Longford near the airport. The 1986 deliveries to this operator included both body styles. An interesting feature of some of the coach-bodied vehicles was the use of a central entrance. The upper illustration shows the bus-bodied version and the lower picture the coach-bodied alternative, both views being taken at Heathrow Terminal Two. (RC both)

Ulsterbus took a single, Plaxton-bodied, example of the B9M to cater for smaller tour groups. The commonality of the chassis features – and therefore spares requirements – with the 'full size' B10M was attractive to large operators such as Ulsterbus. (MB)

Berkhof bodied only two examples of the B9M. Both went to Supreme Coaches at Hadleigh in Essex. The high-floor layout of these coaches make them appear to be appreciably larger than either Plaxton or Van Hool examples. (MB)

Eddie Brown Tours at Helperby in North Yorkshire took a single Van Hool-bodied B9M. With the purchase and operating cost only marginally less than full size coach, operators such as Browns had to be confident of their 'small party' market. (DC)

55

Unusual in being used as a service bus, this B9M/Van Hool of West Coast Motors has arrived in Inveraray from Dunoon to connect with other West Coast services to Oban, Campbeltown and Glasgow. The lengthy journey times on this 'thin route', combined with relatively few stops, made the use of such a high specification vehicle fully justified. (MB)

The contrast in length and height between the seemingly diminutive Allander Travel's B9M and the B10M with a high-floor body and rear saloon of Halcyon of Hull is very marked. The pair are pictured at the coach park at the site of the Battle of Waterloo. (RC)

A late delivery of B9M was to P & J Tours of Uist in Shetland, almost the most northerly operator in the UK. A high quality product was necessary to cater for incoming cruise ship passengers. A cruise ship can be discerned in the background. (MB)

C10M Grand Touring Coach

By 1984 Grand Touring coaches were beginning to appear in Europe. Volvo, as a supplier to the whole of Europe, did not wish to be left out of this small, niche market. Volvo at this time was still wholly committed to the mid-engined layout. All the competing vehicles, however, had a rear-mounted engine, giving cavernous space for luggage. The C10M chassis attempted to combine the best features of both of these layouts by having an underfloor engine, but one mounted as far back towards the rear axle as possible within an extended wheelbase. The long wheelbase gave the descriptor C10M-70.

The coachwork for this very up-market product was built exclusively by the Swiss coachbuilder Ramsier and Jenser to a very high specification.

The result was a superb Grand Touring coach. The cost, however, was prohibitive. In the UK the premium over B10M chassis with a high specification coachwork was about 40%. With both Sweden and Switzerland having high value currencies and both being outside the EU, this was a coach that few operators could afford to use profitably. The UK was not alone in this predicament and only 80 of these splendid vehicles were built before Volvo withdrew the model in December 1986.

Not surprisingly, the UK market absorbed only ten of these magnificent vehicles. The prototype was exhibited at the 1984 Motor Show and then went to Club Cantabrica for running trials from May 1985 for nine months. It was then refurbished and sold to Park' of Hamilton in early 1986. Parks were the only customer to take more than one of these coaches new – and their five examples represented 50% of the UK deliveries. Wallace Arnold took two examples, Seamarks at Luton took one example and renowned operator of very high quality tours, Parry at Cheslyn Hay in the West Midlands, took one example.

The high build quality of this coach is borne out by the long life that many of them exhibited with at least one still engaged in high quality touring some 30 years after it had been built.

The long wheelbase of the C10M meant that the coach was more difficult to manoeuvre than the conventional 12m vehicle with a standard wheelbase, making driving more challenging. The concept of the long wheelbase did, however, emerge again on the B10M-66 designed to give optimum luggage capacity in a 12m vehicle. It was not a popular option and few vehicles with this extended wheelbase entered service in the UK, mainly for National Express duties.

Displayed by Volvo at the 1984 Motor show was B110 CCS. It went to Club Cantabrica at St Albans for running trials until early 1986, when it was refurbished and sold to Parks. At Hamilton it joined the five new C10Ms purchased by that company – the largest UK order for this vehicle type. Once again we see the impressive black livery used by Parks. (MB)

This example of the C10M was supplied new to Wallace Arnold. It was the last C10M delivered in the UK in December 1986. Although very impressed with the vehicle, the high initial cost did not allow further orders. Sold to New Bharat Coaches it is depicted here on a National Express working – lucky passengers! (DC)

Delivered new to Parks this shows the grey/red livery favoured by that operator for a period. The neat rear end styling of the Ramsier and Jenser coachwork is also apparent. The long wheelbase is perhaps over-emphasised. The coach awaits its next duty on Cowcaddens Road in Glasgow, adjacent to the Buchanan Bus Station. (RC)

58

Re-power With Volvo Engines

Volvo was always noticeable in that it did not provide engines and other parts for other manufacturers. It did, however, have a brief foray into the re-power market from mid-1983 onwards. The shortcomings of the Leyland engine in the Leyland National were, by this time, becoming very clear – the 510 engine was noisy, thirsty and, unless very carefully and intensively maintained, unreliable and left many Leyland Nationals at the roadside awaiting the tow truck.

In 1982 Volvo fitted a THD 100 engine into a Leyland National operated by Fife Scottish and altered some of the components to fit around the engine. The result was a rather more refined and reliable Leyland National, but the cost was quite high due to the amount of re-engineering needed. Undeterred, Volvo pressed ahead with a programme offering conversion of the Leyland National and also, perhaps more significantly, the Leyland Tiger.

In the literature claiming to 'Put new life into your Leyland chassis' much was made of the durability of the Volvo engine and the 3,000 hour bench test stating that, '...Engines of other makes have been known to be unusable long before this test is completed' – a very clear swipe at the 510 engine.

Very few Tigers were re-engined in this way as the installation of the Volvo engine required major changes to the chassis frame. However, the Leyland National project gained a steady stream of customers and many were re-engined. When East Lancashire Coachbuilders reworked the original Leyland Nationals and offered the National Greenway, many were fitted with Volvo engines. The Volvo re-engined examples were prized specimens on the second-hand market.

The significance of the installation of the Volvo engine into the Tiger only became apparent once Volvo had taken over Leyland when, using the experience gained in the re-power programme, a large batch of chassis for Ulsterbus were modified at the production stage to take the Volvo TDH 100 engine.

The prototype Leyland National conversion, carried out on a Fife Scottish vehicle, involved a greatly improved air supply to the engine compartment. This was done, crudely, but effectively, by running a duct from the engine bay to the roof. Subsequent conversions used a rather more sophisticated means of improving air flow. (RC)

When East Lancs developed the National Greenway to give operators a rather more refined vehicle many were re-powered with Volvo engines. These buses, along with traditional Leyland Nationals that were re-powered, became prize acquisitions amongst independents and major operators alike, seeking modern, robust and reliable vehicles. (EL)

Trouble-Free Running

While it may cost a little more to install a new Volvo engine than it does to renovate your old engine, it is only a fraction of the cost of a new vehicle. And, with a *new* Volvo engine, your Leyland chassis will, in many respects, be as good as new. It's worth thinking about!
Think about everything you get:

- It is not just an engine replacement - you get additional new components at the same time.

- Future maintenance will be less than after a traditional engine renovation.

- You can look forward to improved profits from undisrupted vehicle use.

- Installation only takes one week - so that should be the maximum downtime for your vehicle.

- Volvo takes responsibility not only for the components, but the quality of the installation work as well - with trained technicians who understand buses and coaches.

- If your vehicle should unexpectedly have problems at home or abroad, there are Volvo workshops close at hand to take care of it - and our Volvo Action Service Europe free phone number will put them on alert for *you*.

The Right Engine for the Job

Reliability is absolutely critical to the profitable operation of any hardworking bus or coach. Any vehicle which has to be taken out of action because of engine problems is bad enough, but a fully loaded tourist
coach with serious roadside problems can have unthinkable economic consequences.
Operators who need to take this into consideration, have put 'Reliability' at the very top of their list of reasons for repowering with a Volvo engine.
The reliability and durability of Volvo's engines are clearly demonstrated in our unique 3,000-hour test. We run an engine non-stop on a test bench, at constant overload, for 3,000 hours - ie: round the clock for four months: engines of other makes have been known to be unusable, long before this test is completed. Today's Volvo engines pass the test by a rassuringly wide margin!
Now, the built-in reliability of a *Volvo* engine can come into its own in a *Leyland* chassis, as Volvo puts its engines to work - at maximum efficiency - in this carefully adapted Leyland environment.

VOLVO

Volvo did not pull any punches in proclaiming the reliability of the Volvo engine over its Leyland counterpart in this publicity literature for the repower programme.

The Leyland Inheritance

Somewhat surprisingly to many observers, Volvo purchased Leyland Bus in March 1988. The Leyland company had been sold out of the unwieldy and heavily loss making British Leyland Motor Holdings to a management buyout only 18 months previously. The buyout team quickly realised that the business they had bought would never flourish – the bus market was depressed and the products that they made were expensive to produce with even the most popular models selling in only modest volumes by European standards.

Volvo inherited a very mixed bag of products ranging from railcars for British Rail to the Swift bus chassis, being built primarily in factories at Workington in Cumbria and Farington in Lancashire.

Railcar production at Workington, a project based on the Leyland National bus, was almost complete when Volvo took over. The railcar suffered from massive warranty claims that sapped resources and occupied a great deal of space at the Workington plant. For future orders British Rail wanted to move from the steel body of the Leyland-built railcar to aluminium – a change that would have required heavy investment at Workington. The decision was quickly made not to stay in the rail building business.

The Leyland Lion, double-deck chassis, was actually built by DAB, a Leyland subsidiary, in Denmark. It had been developed by Leyland as a rather panic stricken reaction to the Citybus but had garnered few orders. It was quickly dropped from the range.

The Leyland Swift was a lightweight chassis, built from Roadrunner truck parts. The Roadrunner truck, however, was part of the Leyland empire sold to DAF. Volvo did not favour buying the bulk of the parts of the Swift from its competitor, DAF. The philosophy of the Swift – a lightweight, limited life vehicle – did not fit into Volvo's framework. For customers who wanted a front-engined chassis Volvo already produced the B6F. Although Swifts continued to be built in 1989 and 1990 after a small batch in 1991 the chassis was dropped.

The Leyland Tiger was a more promising vehicle. At the time of the takeover there were considerable orders from dealers for the chassis. Although it was a competitor to the Volvo B10M it was thought necessary to continue production for the short term. The strange management structure of Volvo in the UK after the takeover allowed Leyland to continue to build Tigers for stock. Many of the stock Tiger chassis proved difficult to sell as operators were fully alive to the possibility of the chassis being discontinued. Nonetheless, Tiger outsold Scania and DAF combined in 1990. A batch of Tigers ordered by Ulsterbus when Leyland was first privatised was delivered in 1991 with Volvo engines – a rather less than subtle hint that Tiger was approaching its death throes. Production finally ceased in 1991 with deliveries extending into 1992.

The Royal Tiger Doyen coach, though quite well received, had proved difficult to market and had sold in very low numbers. It used some expensive propriety parts. It was not difficult to axe this model.

The Olympian was a much more promising chassis. It had consistently been the best selling double-deck chassis in the British Isles ever since its introduction in 1980. It also sold well in overseas markets, especially Hong Kong and Singapore where the three-axle variation had become very popular. It clearly had a future in the Volvo Bus product line-up.

Harrogate and District was one of the few 'large' operators to have the Leyland Swift in stock. Although a high-floor vehicle this neat example gives an idea of the potential for a small bus before the overwhelming arrival of the low-floor midi-bus. (DC)

61

The successor to the Leyland National, being built like its predecessor at Workington, was the Lynx. This semi-integral low-floor rear-engined single-decker had no counterpart in the Volvo range. The Volvo B10R chassis had never been offered in the UK. Lynx, like the Olympian, appeared to have a future. A Volvo engine was soon offered as an option at the same time that the Gardner engine option was dropped. Plans were announced to offer the Lynx underframe to other bodybuilders Europe-wide and to use the Lynx as a basis for a strong export drive. To that end a Lynx underframe was shown in Spain and later in Portugal. In the depressed UK market the Lynx performed quite well, but the underframe development never took place. The fate of the Lynx was determined, however, not wholly by the market, but by the decision by Volvo in December of 1991 to close the Workington factory. The other factor was the development in Sweden of the B10B low-floor chassis for single-deck application. The closure of Workington marked the end of the Lynx.

Volvo also inherited a body building facility at Workington that was building small quantities of bodies to basically ECW designs. It signalled an intention to retain and develop this facility by taking an order in 1991 from Stagecoach for 70 bodies, an order that Alexander's might well have expected to capture. With a huge capacity at Workington, this boded ill for the traditional coachbuilders in the UK. The announcement of the closure of the Workington factory only months later, and before the Stagecoach order could begin to be processed, marked the end of Volvo as a coachbuilder in the UK – and probably salvaged the rest of the bus body building industry!

What had Volvo gained from the expensive purchase of Leyland, if, within four years, it had consolidated all Leyland activity from Farington to Workington and then closed the Workington facility? The major gain was the Olympian and the access to pretty well every British double-deck operator that went with that marque along with access to the important Far Eastern market. It also gained Arlington as an important dealer with excellent track record in and around London. Less obviously, but important in the long run, it acquired a design staff with expertise in independent front suspension and a more general design expertise that came at a much lower price than its Swedish counterpart.

But these gains came at a high price. Railcar warranty costs were very high; the consolidation of production first at Farington and then the relocation to Workington was expensive; the losses incurred in operating the Workington plant were very considerable. Doug Jack suggests that Workington needed to sell about 1,250 chassis a year and the body plant to build about 600 bodies a year just to break even – figures that even in a buoyant market would have been challenging. With a set of buildings that needed modernisation and replacement roof – the roof alone would have cost c£1m – in a climate of low volume sales the decision to close Workington was, however regrettable, inevitable.

The Swift was popular in Jersey where Tantivy Motor Coach Company built up what must be the largest coach fleet on Swift chassis in the British Isles. Pictu... in 2010 these lightly-used vehicles are still in service. (RC)

With the Olympian now in its fold, Volvo gained access to many municipal an... company operators. Volvo's only double-deck offering to them had been the Citybus which did not suit any operator with low-height requirements, or with a long heritage investment in Leyland products. In this way Greater Manchest... became a Volvo customer, as evidenced by this Northern Counties-bodied Olympian. Some of this batch were equipped with sliding ramps for wheelcha... and were used on a normal service between Stalybridge and Oldham whereby wheelchairs could be accommodated without prior arrangements. (STA)

With many hundreds of Atlanteans, Olympians, Leopards, Tigers et al Volvo also inherited a major spares business and rapidly began to improve the performance of this important element of their new empire and make it a useful profit centre. Many operators who had never dealt with Volvo before now became regular customers. Unfortunately, Inter Valley Link did not last very long in the de-regulation environment that was especially tough on small ex-municipal operators. (DC)

The Lynx nearly made it! The chassis was uprated by Volvo for use as stand-alone base for buses and was even marketed in Spain and Portugal. However, it suffered two problems – it was built at the loss-making Workington plant and it was a competitor to the B10B chassis being developed in Sweden. Harrogate and District and the Blazefield Group as a whole became significant Lynx users. (DC)

The Prize! The takeover of Leyland gave Volvo access to the Far Eastern market. Significantly, production of the high value tri-axle Olympian for Hong Kong and Singapore continued in Sweden after the closure of the Irvine factory. (STA)

63

Top of the page and once considered by Leyland as top of its range. With low sales figures, however, and being expensive to build, the Royal Tiger Doyen was quickly axed by Volvo. (DC)

A threatened species! Although the Tiger was given an extension of life following the Volvo takeover, the fact that it competed with the B10M made it inevitable that the model would soon be dropped. Premier Albanian was a proud and committed Tiger operator. (DC)

The Workington Factory. The sign says it all. (STA)

64

Volvo and Express Operations
National Express, Scottish Citylink, Stagecoach Express, Megabus and CIE

Deregulation opened a new era in express coach travel. In England and Wales the old NBC images were swept away to be replaced by a new corporate image – National Express. 20 years ago, in the mid-1990s, National Express was struggling to establish itself and to create a recognisable 'identity' both visually and in terms of consistency of the quality of the journey experience.

Kirkby, the dealers, Volvo, Plaxton and National Express developed the Expressliner to satisfy all of these needs. Based on a B10M chassis the Plaxton body was a development of the Paramount 3500. Internally it was fitted with air conditioning, a toilet and 49-seats in a 12-metre configuration. Externally it was characterised by a blank panel instead of a rear window on which was inscribed the National Express 'flying N' symbol. Kirkby sourced the vehicles and then leased them for a period of five years – the period of the standard National Express contract – to National Express contractors who were paid a marginal bonus to operate this standard coach. At the end of the contract they were refurbished, a rear window installed, and then sold on to the used vehicle market.

In theory all National Express contractors should have leased the Expressliner. In practice this did not always happen. Some contractors objected to leasing – they preferred to purchase the vehicle. Some contractors did not use Volvo chassis and wanted to use Scania, DAF or the Bova integral. Some contractors did not like the Plaxton body and wanted to use Duple or Van Hool. Some contractors used double-deck coaches. Nonetheless the Expressliner set a minimum standard for vehicle performance and body specification. It also marked the beginning of long and positive relationship between Volvo and National Express.

The B10M chassis was followed by the B12B and the B9R. Coachwork moved from Plaxton to Caetano as the preferred supplier and National Express became more insistent on the use of the specified vehicle for contracts. A small number of contractors, notably Parks of Hamilton (and their Plymouth subsidiary, Trathens) and Selwyns in Manchester, continued to use Plaxton bodies for their contracts, using the stylish Elite body to the same internal specification as their Caetano-bodied counterparts.

Following well publicised accidents to Neoplan double-deck coaches National Express determined to withdraw these vehicles. This created the need for a single-deck coach that could carry the same number of passengers. The result was the very impressive, 15m B12B(T) with Plaxton Panther bodywork.

Vehicles on National Express contracts work very hard indeed. Andrew Warrender at Plaxton reckons that one vehicle that came back to Plaxton at the end of a contract had averaged 25mph, day and night, for three years, allowing time for routine servicing. Even if this is a slight exaggeration, it gives a good idea of the extremely high utilisation demanded by contractors operating National Express diagrams. It also says a great deal about the reliability of the various Volvo chassis that have been involved.

In Scotland, after a flurry of activity by enterprising independents, Scottish Citylink performed the same role as National Express, using the extensive Scottish motorway network to challenge railway journey time and frequencies. Like National Express, Scottish Citylink uses contractors to operate its services, chiefly Park's of Hamilton and the ex-SBG companies now owned by Stagecoach, such as Western Buses and Fife. These operators were early converts to the tri-axle B12B(T) with Plaxton Panther body. A more recent, and very successful, development has been Citylink Gold – an upmarket version of the standard Citylink product using the B13R(T) chassis with Plaxton Elite coachwork.

Stagecoach – at one time one of the thrusting independents – grew to takeover ex-SBG companies and used a unified brand, Stagecoach Express, for inter-urban services. These were chiefly in Scotland, but also in pockets of England not served by National Express.

The Expressliner came to be the flagship of National Express. The Rapide specification was originally rather more luxurious than the basic counterpart but soon became the standard. The white livery was initially thought to be a potential disaster by traditional operators, but it quickly became iconic. This example is approaching Morecambe, en route to London via Manchester, with the Lake District skyline behind. (HP)

65

The white livery was, of course, carried by the product of other coachbuilders. Cumberland Motor Services took a batch of Jonckheere-bodied B10M Vehicles for National Express work. 'Go by Coach.com' was an early foray into on-line booking. (HP)

Trathens were, and still are, major contractors to National Express but on their trunk routes from the West Country to London and Scotland used higher capacity vehicles than the Expressliner. This B12B(T) with a twin-deck Berkhof Axial body prepares to leave Paignton for London. It shows a later livery variation. (KM)

Inverness is still 300 miles away as this B12B(T) with Plaxton Panther body pauses at the northbound Tebay service area. Parks of Hamilton gained very high utilisation from their vehicles which are distinguishable by their registration sequences in the HSK/LSK series – passed from one intake of vehicles to the next. (JAS)

66

In Ireland, in the 1990s, the state owned operator, CIE, began to look at the express market when the poor quality of the railway operation, and the fact that it served only limited parts of the country, suggested that there was a major opportunity. This, combined with a rise in the standard of living that encouraged more travel, road improvement programmes and early motorway construction, led CIE to seek a standard coach, much like National Express, that would offer a consistent and reliable service across the country. The result was, again, a B10M/Plaxton combination for mid-1990 deliveries and with Caetano coachwork for late 1990s deliveries. The millennium saw a change to B7R/Plaxton.

Stagecoach's Megabus has had a briefer history and has evolved a great deal from the initial concept. From being a very cheap and very basic means of competing for stage services in a post-deregulation environment, it has evolved into an innovative, long distance, value for money, coaching operation. Megabus, like National Express and Citylink, requires a very high utilisation of its assets to be a successful economic operation. The earning capacity of a 65-seat coach, despite marginally higher running costs and an initial higher capital cost over a 12m vehicle, were very attractive. Megabus, too, took to the B12B(T), and later B13R(T), chassis with the Plaxton Panther body.

An excellent example of both innovation and thrift at Megabus was the decision to trial overnight sleeper services from Scotland to London using a batch of B10M articulated vehicles originally operated by Fife Scottish. The vehicles were already twelve years old, with high mileages gained on Fife Express services, yet they performed so well that Megabus ordered a fleet of new B11R/Plaxton Elite*i* coaches for this new venture. This is a tribute to the original quality of the chassis and body, and to the quality of the maintenance they had received.

Megabus also operates a number of Van Hool integral vehicles to semi-twin deck layout, but these are being challenged by Plaxton's new Elite*i* body placed on the Volvo B11R chassis – a move doubtless aided by the fact that Sir Brian Souter is a major shareholder in both Stagecoach and Alexander Dennis, the parent company of Plaxton. This combination allowed Plaxton to re-enter the European market for the first time in 20 years, as Polski Bus (which just happens to be another enterprise in which Sir Brian is deeply involved!) ordered 20 of this combination which were delivered in 2014.

Volvo has come to overwhelmingly dominate the Express Coach market in the UK and it has become an important part of the 'mix' of vehicles supplied to the UK and Ireland.

When Parks took over Trathens, new deliveries arrived with the distinctive Park's registration. A B9R with Plaxton's Elite body is parked-up at Plymouth. (KM)

The advent of the Disability Discrimination Act has required coachbuilders to incorporate lifts into their new vehicles. Here the lift in HSK 645 is tested at Trathen's base in Plymouth. National Express had carried out pioneering work in this area by fitting lifts to extended B10M with Plaxton bodies to operate between Bristol and London. (KM)

The Caetano body has become synonymous with National Express usually mounted on a B9R chassis. This standard vehicle enabled both large and small operators to bid for National Express work from a 'level playing field'. Operators would frequently lease the vehicle for the duration of the National Express contract. This example is operated by The Travellers Choice at Carnforth and is seen entering Hanley bus station en-route from Manchester to Bournemouth. (RC)

The full length of the Plaxton Panther-bodied B12B(T) is apparent from this picture. There is a rear steer facility that makes these vehicles surprisingly manoeuvrable. The aggressive pricing policy of Megabus is apparent to all other road users as well as pedestrians. (JAS)

Berrys was one of the more successful independents to compete with National Express, and continues to do so today. A high-floor Van Hool Alizee with a rear cabin mounted on a B10M(T) waits at Tiverton to depart 'Superfast' to London. (RC)

68

In Scotland Newtons at Dingwall joined forces with Allander Travel at Milngavie to operate an express service from Glasgow to Inverness. Newton invested in two impressive B10M(T) with Plaxton bodies for this service. Within twelve months of purchasing these vehicles Newton sold out to City link, but in their new blue and yellow livery these coaches were far less impressive. (JS)

Allander's contribution to the joint service took the form of Van Hool Alizee-bodied B10M, seen here awaiting departure from Glasgow. (RC)

In the early days of de-regulation, Stagecoach focussed on serving the oil rich city of Aberdeen, linking it to the Central Belt of Scotland and to London. A Plaxton Paramount-bodied B10M is seen at the euphemistically named 'Parks City Coach Station' in Glasgow. From this beginning the mighty Stagecoach empire grew! (RC)

69

Once Stagecoach had purchased a number of ex-SBG subsidiaries it became possible to develop the Stagecoach Express brand, linking many secondary towns to the major cities of Glasgow and Edinburgh. A Plaxton Premier-bodied B10M in an early version of the Stagecoach Express livery, awaits departure for Fife from Glasgow's Buchanan Bus Station. (RC)

Success led to greater demand for seats and because low bridges prevented the use of double-deck vehicles Stagecoach purchased a batch of articulated B10M – B10MA – mainly with Plaxton bodies, but two had Jonckheere coachwork. These vehicles worked from Glasgow and Edinburgh into Fife and from Glasgow to Irvine and Ayr. A Jonckheere-bodied example leaves Glasgow Buchanan for Irvine. (MB)

Citylink has had a long 'on-off' relationship with West Coast Motors, but it has always made good commercial sense to have through ticketing. Here, in the early days of Citylink, two immaculate West Coast Motors Jonckheere-bodied B10Ms sit at Glasgow Buchanan Bus Station ready to depart for Campbeltown and Oban respectively. The livery is 'early Citylink'. (RC)

70

Heavy passenger loadings led Citylink also to move to the 15-metre tri-axle combination. This B12B(T)/Plaxton of Western Buses awaits entry to Buchanan Bus Station in Glasgow before setting off for Birmingham on a National Express diagram. (DC)

Citylink ran into problems with the Monopolies and Mergers Commission and was forced to divest some of its interests. These interests were taken over by Park's of Hamilton, one of Citylink's major contractors, and although the livery and the vehicles remained the same the branding was that of Park's rather than Citylink. A Plaxton-bodied B13R(T) demonstrates the new shareholder in the Citylink enterprise. (JS)

The English version of Stagecoach Express has, with some notable exceptions such as Oxford-Cambridge, been Megabus. Similar vehicles – Plaxton-bodied B12B(T) and B13B(T) – but a different livery and a more competitive philosophy. The need for high utilisation is even more imperative with lower fares. This Megabus leaves Manchester for Plymouth. (RC)

71

The success of Megubus led to that operation becoming the lead customer for the new Plaxton Elitei coachwork on the Volvo B11R chassis. This highly sophisticated vehicle, used on overnight and daytime Scotland-London services, is a worthy successor to the Alexander-bodied B10M 'London' coaches. (PL)

In Ireland the nationalised Bus Eireann dominates the provision of express services. In the early years of the new Millennium the operator invested heavily in fleet renewal, primarily using Volvo chassis. This example, a B12B with a Caetano body, competes with the railway from Wexford to Dublin. (MB)

In 2004 a batch of B12B with Sunsundegui Sideral bodies was taken into stock. They had a more generous seat pitch, accommodating only 47, for use on longer journeys. This example leaves no doubt as to its route. (MB)

Challenges to the Bus Eireann dominance have, however, had some success. The regulators have awarded the right to operate express services to an increasing number of independents, though deregulation is still a long way off. An early challenger was McGinley at Gortahork in Co. Donegal who purchased this Plaxton-bodied B10M new to operate from Donegal into Dublin. (MB)

Nestor Link competed with Bus Eireann on the Galway link to Dublin, with the added attraction of serving Dublin airport directly. This B12B with Sunsundegui coachwork operates on the most contested express route in Ireland. (MB)

Comfort-Delgro, owner of Scottish Citylink, also established Irish Citylink using the same principle of contracting out the actual operation of services. Using a B12B with Volvo coachwork, this example operated by Callinan Coaches of Claregalway leaves Dublin for its home territory. The livery borrows heavily from Scottish Citylink, with a touch of the Megabus. (MB)

73

First Group pushed into the Irish market by operating services direct to Dublin airport from Dublin and south of the City. Aircoach is the appropriate trading name of Last Passive Ltd. An initial fleet of Setras was replaced by a fleet of B12B(T) with Jonckheere coachwork, one of which is seen above in Dublin's O'Connell Street. (MB)

The B12B/Sunsundegui combination also found favour with Ulsterbus who used this example on the cross border express service from Belfast to Dublin. (MB)

B12 Coach Chassis

The B12-60 chassis was Volvo's first foray into rear-engines. A vertical 12-litre engine, developing up to 405bhp, was fitted as befitted a heavyweight chassis that was designed primarily to be a tri-axle vehicle with double-deck coachwork. A two axle version was available and in left hand drive form was used by Plaxton to enter the European market where it sold over 20 vehicles after an appearance at the Paris Motor Show – details of these sales remain remarkably scarce and photographs even more so.

The first UK deliveries took place in 1993 with Van Hool coachwork to Trathen in Plymouth and to Berry at Taunton. As might be expected, sales were steady rather than spectacular. The vehicles tended to be used on gruelling National Express diagrams in which vehicles travelled the length and breadth of the country, stopping only for fuel and routine maintenance. The 'costa run' was also a popular use for these vehicles, exemplified by the four Berkhof-bodied examples purchased by Ferris in South Wales. Bebbs at Llantwit Fardre, also in South Wales, were amongst the most regular customer taking three separate batches with Jonckheere bodies for National Express duties, with Trathen and Park's of Hamilton also taking repeat deliveries.

For the 1997 season the chassis was updated (and re-titled B12(T)) and Van Hool exhibited an example on their stand at the 1997 Bus and Coach show. This vehicle caused quite a stir as it was liveried for, and sold to, Stobart of Carlisle, a major force in the UK trucking world but who, previously, had shown no interest in the coaching business. Many thought that this marked the beginning of a new force in coaching, but this was not the case and the vehicle was sold after a relatively short period with Stobart. The B12 also gave Volvo entry to the world of pop music when two examples were sold to Buddens at Woodfalls and one to Bromwich at Southam in Warwickshire, all for use by musical groups on tour. A small batch of right hand drive vehicles was supplied to Citybus in Hong Kong with Jonckheere 73-seat coachwork.

As a single-deck vehicle with a high-floor body it offered vast amounts of luggage space for incoming tourists and for airport transfers, First Beeline taking seven Plaxton-bodied examples for the latter purpose. This was not a high volume chassis, however, and it was withdrawn in 2001 to be replaced with uprated versions of the B12B(T) chassis. The last deliveries were to Park's of Hamilton in the early months of 2002.

It was noticeable that the coach building was dominated by Van Hool, Jonckheere and Berkhof with their double-deck coach designs. Plaxton built only on the single-deck version of the chassis.

The somewhat angular and upright design of Van Hool double-deck coachwork was the most common on the B12 chassis – seen here on one of Trathen's vehicles. Following the takeover of Trathens by Park's this vehicle was intended, and liveried, for Scottish Citylink work – but was never actually used for that purpose. (KM)

Dodsworth's Plaxton-bodied single-deck B12 was completed to a very high specification – 'The Ultimate' as it claimed. Used for touring groups where luggage capacity was important, the Excalibur body was an impressive example of the UK coachbuilders' art. (MB)

As a heavyweight chassis B12 was expected to work hard – including hauling a trailer. Manipulating a 12-metre coach with a trailer is no easy task. The photographer wisely practiced in Saltash business park before venturing to take Trathen's Van Hool-bodied example to places where mistakes would be difficult to rectify. (KM)

A late model B12(T) when single-deck production dominated, this Plaxton-bodied example was new to Nottingham City Transport before migrating to Eire. Does the '380' refer to an engine capability or the height of the vehicle? (MB)

The 'Band Bus' was a feature of the 1990s, taking pop groups from gig to gig around the UK and Europe. These vehicles were lavishly fitted with bunks and all other comforts. Trathens at Plymouth had a small fleet of Star Rider coaches, including LSK 615 seen at the Plymouth base. (KM)

Facing page:

Bebb's at Llantwit Fardre took several single-deck batches of B12 for National Express operation to Heathrow and London, where luggage capacity was an important consideration. These coaches found a ready second-hand market. This Jonckheere-bodied vehicle with Wright Bros at Nenthead is a classic example. (MB)

Dukes Travel, in the Forest of Dean, was another operator eager to take an ex-Bebb vehicle and use it for touring purposes. The example in the lower illustration now carries a cherished registration. (JAS)

76

WRIGHT BROS.
WRIGHT BROS.
VDL JONCKHEERE
M29 HNY

DUKES TRAVEL
traveland
P&O Cruises
0800-074 3430
traveland
Go By Dukes
H7 GBD

B12M and B12B Coach Chassis

By 2000 the market leading B10M had been in production for over two decades and needed to be upgraded. In that time over 10,000 B10M chassis had been delivered in the UK and Ireland – almost 20% of total B10M deliveries of 52,000 chassis worldwide. The result of the upgrading process was the B12M that was launched at ExpoCoach 2000 in September 2000.

Volvo had developed a totally new platform for coach and bus application – the TX platform. This had been under development for about two years in Sweden and had had early testing and operational experience in Sweden. The major difference from B10M was the use of a stainless steel chassis frame that was laser cut and then, as with B10M, welded. The engine was the relatively new D12 that had been well tested in the trucking environment – this, as the model designation implied, was a 12-litre unit that had been used in vertical form in the B12 chassis (see page 75). The engine fully satisfied Euro 3 requirements whilst developing 340bhp. Gearboxes from both ZF and Volvo were available and retarder packages were fitted as standard. There was also a totally new instrument panel which incorporated a great deal of diagnostic equipment and fully adjustable steering rake and instrument binnacle. Service intervals were extended to c30,000 miles. The whole package came in slightly lighter than its predecessor.

Volvo took the somewhat unusual step in 2001 of supplying twelve chassis to selected operators for a twelve month period to obtain UK operator feedback before a full delivery schedule was undertaken in 2002. The UK was a key market and Volvo could not afford to make mistakes. These early production models went to, amongst others, Flights, Wallace Arnold, Dunn Line and Kenzies. Chassis number 102-113 were used for this purpose. In the twelve months that these vehicles were being assessed Volvo delivered over 350 further B10M chassis.

Not surprisingly, bodybuilders were anxious to body the new chassis and it was initially available with a choice of Jonckheere, Van Hool, Berkhof, Caetano and Plaxton bodywork along with a newcomer to the UK market Sunsundegui of Spain brought in by Volvo as a potential replacement for Plaxton, which was then in severe trouble and facing the threat of closure. With some relaxation of the regulations over length, some vehicles were built to 12.8-metre configuration. All B12M chassis were built at Boras and all UK deliveries were two axle machines and, as a result, no double-deck-bodies appeared on this chassis. Double-deck vehicles at this time were catered for by the B12 chassis.

With a more 'level playing field' in the market Volvo used the B12M to penetrate new markets, such as the ex-NBC companies and the new groups that emerged from the consolidation of the operating companies. Shearings, Wallace Arnold and Park's continued to feature strongly in deliveries but First Group companies also began to feature in the schedule. An interesting trio of vehicles was delivered to First Bristol in late 2002, featuring in-built wheelchair access to their Plaxton bodies – the first vehicles to be so fitted, and used on express services from Bristol to London. These vehicles operated under special dispensation as they were the first 12.8m vehicles in the country. They became the forerunner of many more. Although, as was pointed out at the time, the additional cost and the loss of seating would have made it cheaper to send every disabled person by taxi, mobility for disabled people was high on the political agenda and slowly all National Express contractors had to comply with the new regulations.

The increased demand for high quality travel led a small number of operators, chiefly Park's of Hamilton and Wallace Arnold (with its Grand Tourer sales pitch and GT registrations) to specify very luxurious 36-seat configurations with either Jonckheere or Plaxton coachwork. It was noticeable that very few operators specified the maximum seating capacity of 57, 53 being the norm.

Competition for Volvo now came from the European mainland. Setra and Van Hool offered integral coaches, along with Bova. Scania had linked with Irizar. DAF had abandoned the mid-engined configuration for a rear-engined product. Mercedes Benz had a fledgling organisation. All of the competitors were a rear-engined product with the resulting luggage capacity being greatly increased. With more skilfully engineered vehicles the Volvo claim that the mid-engined layout was safer and more efficient began to loose ground. Indeed, Volvo itself had already 'sold the pass' over the mid-engined configuration with the B12. The B12 had illustrated that the rear-engine configuration could cope with the most demanding schedules and the heaviest coachwork.

Although the majority of B12M chassis were bodied by Plaxton, other coachbuilders featured more strongly than on B10M. Jonckheere, especially, built a sound reputation for a well built, well finished product. Halpenny Travel added this Jonckheere-bodied example, left, to its Volvo dominated fleet. (MB)

78

Above: Before Longstaff at Mirfield decided to leave the coaching business and focus on bus operation, the company purchased this Van Hool-bodied B12M and used a private registration plate. Here the vehicle is seen awaiting its returning passengers at Ness Gardens on the Wirral. (JAS)

Exemplifying the attempts by the major tour groups to attract more affluent and more discerning clients, Wallace Arnold introduced the Grand Tourer fitted with only 46 seats, air conditioning and other 'luxury' features. This Jonckheere-bodied B12M awaits its clients at South Mimms Services. (KM)

In order to offer competition to the rear-engine adversaries, Volvo offered the B12B for the 2002 season. This was, effectively, a B12M, but with a rear engine rather than an underfloor engine. Knowing that many operators had maintenance facilities that were geared up to underfloor engines, Volvo sold the B12B as being a complimentary chassis to B12M and for two or three years the sales were about equal in number. By 2006, however, sales of B12M were declining although loyal adherents to the configuration, chief amongst them Park's of Hamilton, continued to purchase examples in 2007 and 2008. By 2009 the last B12M had left the Boras factory. Pulhams, at Bourton on the Water in the Cotswolds, claimed the last B12M to enter service, matching its record with the B10M almost a decade earlier.

After six years of being offered for the heaviest coachwork and the most arduous duties, the B12 chassis was dropped from the UK market in 2002. It was replaced by B12B. The first tri-axle B12BTs were delivered in 2003 to South Wales operators Ferris at Nantgarw and Thomas at Porth, all with Berkhof double-deck bodies. Changes to vehicle length regulations allowed longer vehicles on two axles, up to 13.8m, and even longer vehicles, up to 15m, on three axles. B12B was able to cope with all of the demands resulting from these changes.

One of the more interesting orders for B12B came to meet the demands of Scottish Citylink who did not wish to use double-deck vehicles in express services, yet needed additional capacity to cope with growing demand. No less than 40 B12BT with Plaxton bodies were ordered by Park's and Western Scottish. Plaxton had speedily to extend paint booths to take these 15-metre (the newly allowed maximum length), 65-seat vehicles. These impressive vehicles, equipped with rear steer, soon became a common sight on Motorways in Scotland and England, especially as later orders went to Trathens for National Express services from the West Country. In Ireland an equally impressive set of vehicles were supplied to Last Passive, operating as Aircoach, at Dublin with Jonckheere bodies for express services to and from Dublin airport. Two Scottish holiday companies also standardised on the B12BT to carry English passengers to Scottish destinations – Lochs and Glens chose Jonckheere coachwork, whilst Highland Heritage chose Van Hool.

During the lifetime of the B12B Volvo began to offer its own coachwork built to a very high specification in Poland. By 2007 Poland had recently joined the European Union and offered a lower cost base for skilled manpower. This was a marked contrast to the very high cost base for Ramsier and Jenser in

Switzerland that had contributed to the lack of success of the C10M. Beginning in early 2008, Volvo bodies were supplied to the UK and Ireland, in a steady trickle rather than a flood, the market continuing to be dominated by Plaxton, Van Hool and Jonckheere. National Express were beginning their long relationship with Caetano and a number of chassis appeared with this manufacturers bodies operating for National Express contractors.

The development of the Irish economy meant that during the 1990s that market began to feature more prominently in Volvo sales. The pressures on the Irish state bus and coach company, CIE, to 'liberalise' meant that a number of express services were operated on a contract basis by private companies. The Volvo-bodied B12BT became a popular work horse on these services.

B12M and B12B, although thoroughbred machines that were reliable and economic to operate, never quite managed to gain the affection of the operators that B58 and especially B10M had done. This was probably because it was really the first Volvo chassis that had been dependent upon electronics and for which a 'spanner and a hammer' were wholly inadequate and inappropriate tools. The generation of smaller operators who had developed their businesses in a different era found this a difficult transition. There was also a great deal more variety available to the operator – both in terms of chassis and coachwork – most of which had 'caught up' with Volvo in terms of reliability – and most of which had begun to emulate Volvo's ideas of customer satisfaction and support.

With ever encroaching legislation and with rising competition, Volvo began to develop a replacement chassis for the B12B that emerged in two forms – in 2011 as the B13R for heavyweight configurations, and the B9R in 2008 to fill the remainder of the needs that had been satisfied by B12B.

In Yorkshire, Stephensons at Easingwold served a more rural population. Another variation in livery style indicates how versatile the Panther coachwork could be. The ducks on the green clearly have a special place in Easingwold life. (DC)

80

Plaxton's Panther coachwork graced many B12M chassis. Lakeside at Ellesmere in Cheshire took a very traditional livery and by modernising it made it fit the lines of the Panther body extremely well. (DC)

Lloyds at Machynlleth has only a small coach fleet, including this B12M with familiar Plaxton body. It is parked up at the top of Penglais Hill awaiting the call to collect passengers from Aberystwyth. (RC)

Eddie Brown Tours at Helperby in Yorkshire had long favoured Volvo chassis when this Plaxton-bodied example joined the fleet. Lower case lettering and 'waves' in the livery were both designed to project a more modern image. (DC)

81

In 2014 Roy McCarthy Coaches became the first operator to take the Plaxton Leopard-bodied B8R to Euro 6 specification. It had been preceded by a number of Volvo/Plaxton coaches, including this B12B Plaxton Paragon example pictured at Gawsworth near McCarthy's home town of Macclesfield. (PL)

The B12B was almost indistinguishable visually from B12M – the rear radiator position being the only real guide. Andrews at Tideswell in the Derbyshire Peak District enjoys a rural location, as evidenced from this picture, but is almost equidistant from the population centres of Manchester, Sheffield and the East Midlands that keeps a predominantly Volvo fleet busy. A new B12B poses only yards from the depot. (DC)

Acklams Coaches of Beverley in North Yorkshire are proud of their community base and their coaches have traditionally carried a depiction of feature of the town – in this case the North Bar. This is another B12B/Plaxton Panther. (DC)

Taff Valley Coaches must be one of the very few UK mainland operators to letter their vehicles in a language other than English – in this case in Welsh. Serving a strong Welsh speaking community this makes good business sense. A B12B/Plaxton Panther sits outside the depot. (DC)

With B12B, Volvo's own coachwork began to emerge. It was marketed as a 'top of the range' product at a premium price. Dudley's at Radford in Worcestershire took this example in March 2010. The styling is restrained and designed to be 'timeless'. It is seen here at the UK Coach Rally. (KM)

83

Volvo also offered Sunsundegui coachwork on the B12B. This was, essentially, a no-frills, hardwearing bodywork suitable for short distance private hire and express work. Ulsterbus took a batch in 2008. One of that batch is seen four years later operating for Stagecoach Events at the Olympic Games. (MB)

With a competitive price tag, the Sunsundegui body was attractive to Irish operators beginning to re-equip their fleets as the Irish economy expanded. Lally's 2004 example stands in its home town of Galway. Threats to coach operators parking for longer periods than a local authority decides on are as common in Eire as the UK. (MB)

The B12B with Plaxton coachwork found favour for touring work north of the border. Ulsterbus took small batch to a high specification for touring work in 2005 and 2006, amongst them DEZ 4115 of the 2005 batch. (MB)

84

Wallace Arnold and Shearings were both long-term users of the Volvo chassis, with various coachbuilders. When Shearings took over the Wallace Arnold operation it instituted a 'mixed' livery, but finally opted for a new, darker shade of blue. These Van Hool-bodied B12Bs standing at the foot of the fearsome Countessbury Hill, Lynmouth, in North Devon demonstrate the change – with the new livery and wholly Shearings branding on the further vehicle. (JAS)

With relaxation of the weight and length restrictions for coaches the tri-axle version of the B12B – B12BT – enabled coachbuilders to construct larger and heavier vehicles. There are no less than three major Kavanagh operations at Urlingford in County Kilkenny, together offering over 250 coaches. This example, seen on incoming tour work in Dublin, is a B12BT with Van Hool coachwork operated by Pierce Kavanagh, the smallest of the trio. (MB)

Park's of Hamilton, always to the forefront, received high specification double-deck Jonckheere coachwork on Volvo B12BT. Despite toilets and galleys 'comfort stops' were still required to comply with driver's hours regulations. KSK 983 awaits the return of its passengers. (KM)

85

Whilst it is not thought that B12BT pulled trailers (see B12, page 76) they were able to carry a rear ski box within the overall permitted length. This Jonckheere-bodied example with Park's of Hamilton emerged as a most impressive machine, with a performance to match its load carrying capability. This vehicle is notable in not using one of Park's KSK/LSK registration that, as previously mentioned, are carried forward from generation to generation. (KM)

Highland Heritage is one of two companies that owns its own fleet of coaches to feed holidaymakers from all over the UK to its hotels in Scotland. The 15-metre, Van Hool-bodied B12BT was able to offer the comfort and reliability needed for the sometimes lengthy journeys to the Scottish Highlands. (MB)

The other operator to follow this model is Lochs and Glens Holidays. From modest beginnings this operation has expanded, and with it the fleet of Jonckheere-bodied B12BT. The coaches are used to bring holidaymakers to Scotland and then to carry them to a wide variety of attractions within Scotland. Here, no less than four of these expensive machines await passengers in Dunoon who will arrive on the paddle steamer 'Waverley'. (RC)

86

As one of the initiators of the Elite body style, Logan at Dunloy in County Antrim, was an early operator to take delivery of a B12BT with the Elite body. This high specification vehicle is seen operating on charter to CIE Tours. (DC)

First Group has only a small presence in the Republic of Ireland, mainly the Aircoach operation to and from Dublin Airport, established once limited deregulation allowed this. These impressive B12BT/Jonckheere coaches are a familiar sight on O'Connell Street, Dublin, as they pass through to serve southside destinations. (RC)

The B12BT, initially with Plaxton's Paragon body and then with the stylish Elite body, became a favourite workhorse for Citylink, Park's and Stagecoach in Scotland. The elegant lines of the Elite body fit well on the 15-metre chassis. (JS)

87

'Cabins' on Two and Three Axles

The precision jig welded frame and air suspension on the B10M chassis led to some interesting developments in bodywork. In 1991, only twelve months after the chassis was introduced, Jonckheere introduced a body style that was to become popular with operators on the 'sun run' to Spain, to Swiss ski resorts and similar destinations.

The Jonckheere P90 body combined a high-floor main deck with a small rear cabin beneath the high-floor and behind the rear axle, but still on a two axle chassis. After some debate with the importers, Roeslare Sales, these vehicles were classified by the Ministry of Transport as double-deckers. This brought with it the advantage of a less demanding tilt test, but the downside of requiring a driver to have a double-deck licence. Van Hool and Berkhof followed suit in placing similar bodies on the 2-axle chassis. With no rear window the 'cabin' must have been a most claustrophobic environment in which to travel long distances.

The P90 body and its look-alikes created a problem with weight distribution. With a full complement of passengers and their luggage, a kitchen, toilet, double glazing etc, despite the advantage of the mid-engine layout, it was difficult to remain within the law on axle weights.

The solution for Volvo was to fit a third axle. This was already done in Sweden where lengths of up to 15m were allowed with a third axle. In the UK the third axle solved the problem of weight whilst remaining within the 12m overall length. The wheelbase was shortened and a third axle placed in the position of the second axle on a two-axle vehicle. The standard engine was uprated to 276bhp and charge cooling was introduced (a means of improving the power rating and fuel consumption, as well as reducing exhaust emissions) the B10MT ('T' for tandem) or B10M-53 was born.

The advent of the tri-axle variation allowed Jonckheere, Van Hool and Berkhof to build with greater confidence, and it also tempted Plaxton into the market with the specifically designed 4000RS body. The double-deck body and the cavernous luggage space encouraged the use of the B10MT – and later the B12MT – on airport shuttle and longer distance express services. Flights of Birmingham developed a network of express services serving airports across England using both Jonckheere and Plaxton bodies. Newtons at Dingwall used two Plaxton-bodied examples in a striking livery before selling-out to Scottish Citylink. Berry at Taunton used Plaxton-bodied example and Park's operated a number of Jonckheere examples. The ability to place both double and single-deck bodies on the same chassis was exploited by Western SMT who ordered a batch of B10M with both single and double-deck bodies by Berkhof.

The advent of the B12B(T) rear-engined chassis allowed a much more civilised arrangement, placing a lower saloon in front of the rear axle, creating, effectively, a double-decked vehicle.

'One of Guards'. The simple livery makes this an impressive looking coach and epitomises the Executive use to which many of the Jonckheere P90 vehicles were put. The blue band masks the driver's compartment door – a cubby hole in which a second driver was supposed to rest when not driving. Even more claustrophobic than the rear 'cabin'! (DC)

This award winning vehicle of Clarkes at Loughborough shows the neat lines of the Jonckheere Jubilee P90 body. In this executive application, where maximising the number of seats was not the imperative, the rear 'cabin' was used as a lounge area. (DC)

Here we clearly see the rear cabin on the Plaxton-bodied B10M. This configuration was only possible on an underfloor-engined chassis. This vehicle represented a major investment for a relatively small West Wales operator. It was intended to take holidaymakers to the south of France before the advent of low cost airlines. (DC)

Berkhof's Emperor bodywork followed the same pattern as the Jonckheere design. This Western Scottish example was one of very few built by Berkhof for the UK market. The 'cabin' had to have both a nearside and offside doorway in order to satisfy the safety regulations. (RC)

89

Trathens also took delivery of Van Hool's Astral bodywork to the same basic layout. The 'Starider' brand was deliberately pitched at up-market clients in order to justify the high tariffs charged to use this vehicle. (DC)

The tri-axle chassis allowed for a greater margin for error on axle loading and also allowed the coachbuilder to produce a virtually double-deck coach. The Plaxton 4000RS design was especially impressive. Used primarily for express work, this example of Flight's of Birmingham is being used for tour work and is seen at Drymen, close to Loch Lomond. (RC)

The vast luggage capacity of these vehicles – essential when used for express work or for incoming tourists – is readily appreciated on this Van Hool-bodied B10MT Citylink coach leaving Birmingham for Glasgow. (DC)

The B12B(T) chassis enabled coachbuilders to provide a rather more civilised forward-facing downstairs saloon. Berry's of Taunton took full advantage of the opportunity on this Van Hool-bodied example, used on their London-West Country service. (MB)

Although not having a rear saloon, this unique Ajokki-bodied coach made full use of the tri-axle configuration to maximise luggage space. Although it was a splendid coach the high cost of the Finnish construction meant that this remained the only example in the UK. (DC)

B7R Coach Chassis

B10M, B12M and B12B were regarded as heavyweight chassis. Volvo had no offering in the lighter weight, cheaper end of the market where the Dennis Javelin had had some success in filling the gap left by the withdrawal of Ford and Bedford from the market. B7R was designed to fill that space.

Fitted with a D7 engine giving 290bhp, B7R was a simple, straight frame, rear engine chassis, designed by Volvo to fit all of its markets, from dirt roads in Africa to motorways in Europe. The chassis was launched in South Africa in 1998 and became available in GB at the same time. Volvo's intention was to sell it as a 'package' with a Plaxton Prima body developed specifically for the chassis, giving only a limited choice of specifications so that it would be simple to build and necessitate holding only a limited range of spares.

It has been successful in its role. Almost 1,000 chassis have been sold in the UK and Ireland from its launch in 1998 to 2013, the great majority with the Plaxton body. The chassis has enjoyed particular success with Stagecoach and First Group who have used it to offer coach seating and facilities on what might once have been dual-purpose inter-urban routes. This has been especially noticeable in Scotland where the lower initial capital outlay enabled Stagecoach to offer very attractive vehicles on lengthy routes into the Scottish Highlands, later deliveries even having lifts fitted. Bus Eireann used a batch of over 50 vehicles for the same purpose in Ireland. The largest single customer was Ulsterbus who took 200 with Wright bodies, seating 66 and having disabled access, for school duties. Some 45 Plaxton-bodied chassis went to the Ministry of Defence.

In 2004 Wright produced a very interesting prototype of what it called the 'Commuter Coach' on a modified B7R chassis. By dropping the front axle back it was able to create a low level 'platform' for a wheelchair and carer as well as 49-seats in a main, normal level saloon. It produced two other demonstrators and two further examples for Dumfries and Galloway Council that were operated by Western Buses on the Carlisle-Stranraer corridor. The idea was overtaken by the development of more effective lifts giving disabled access to high-floor coaches.

Small numbers of chassis were bodied by Jonckheere after 2002 for those operators wanting a more upmarket image and Volvo offered the Sunsundegui body for the 2005 season onwards. During its twilight period in 2012 and 2013 Sunsundegui bodied a number of shorter wheelbase B7R chassis, Volvo having determined that once again there was market for a smaller, full specification coach – a 'sort of' replacement for the B10M-48 (B9M) of 25 years previously.

Encouraged by the need for tendered school transport, many of the B7Rs were given 3+2 seating to give a capacity of 66-70. One operator in particular, Woodstones of Kidderminster, came back year after year for two coaches to this specification.

B7R was a useful workhorse. With very light controls it was regarded as very suitable for an increasing cohort of lady drivers. It filled a useful niche in many operators range of vehicles. Without fuss and fanfare 'it did what it said on the tin'.

The UK launch customer for B7R was James Bevan at Lydney in the Forest of Dean. This was a clever choice as it signalled that this was a chassis for small operators. This image was supported by the basic specification Plaxton body as the standard option – though uprating was always possible. (RC)

The B7R chassis was simple and rugged. It is seen here with a straight frame, as it was introduced. However, it soon became available with a divided frame to give more luggage space between the wheelbase. (DJ)

Prospect Coaches of Lye in the West Midlands took two examples in order to celebrate their Golden Anniversary. The destination displays made these vehicles suitable for a wide variety of purposes including National Express duplication. (DC)

Smith of Ledbury in Herefordshire was a typical small operator attracted to B7R with its lower capital cost and a good all-round capability. It is seen here in its home town. (DC)

A very loyal B7R customer was Woodstone of Kidderminster who used his vehicles for both touring and schools work – the latter to a (3+2) 70-seat configuration. Woodstones were one of the first operators to move to Euro 6 and adopt the B8R platform. (DC)

93

The market for a small, but full-specification, coach has always been limited as the cost was little less than a full-size model. Nonetheless, Volvo produced a 'mini' B7R with Sunsundegui coachwork to satisfy this market, with some success. This example, with Doigs of Glasgow, sits in the car park at Loch Lomond Park on a not untypical grey and damp day in 2000. (RC)

In 2004 Dualway of Rathcool in Eire took delivery of one of only two Jonckheere-bodied B7R delivered new to the Republic. The Modulo body was the manufacturer's 'entry level' design and fitted with the basic philosophy of the B7R chassis. (MB)

The final Plaxton-bodied full-size B7R produced was delivered to another customer loyal to this marque – Henry Cooper at Ashington in Northumberland. (DC)

Posed on top of the Malvern Hills in Worcestershire (just!) is a Plaxton-bodied B7R new to Newbury Coaches. The rural location tends to emphasise the perceived versatility of the B7R chassis making it suitable – and affordable – to the well-run rural operator. (DC)

By contrast the largest single order for the B7R came from Ulsterbus for 200 chassis to be bodied by Wrights for school duties. Modified version of the Commuter body – which it designated Skolarbus - with a nearside resulting in rather 'boxy' end product that was appreciably higher than their standard body – demonstrated by the 'normal height' Scania alongside. (MB)

Although widely reported as being on B7RLE chassis, the Wright Commuter body – designed to accommodate less mobile passengers on a low platform with a coach style main interior – could easily have been on a modified B7R chassis with a set back front axle. Only five of these vehicles were built, but the principle was used by Plaxton for their Elite body. The two vehicles operated by Stagecoach were inspired by Dumfries and Galloway Council and operate the Dumfries-Stranraer service. The lengthy front overhang to accommodate seats behind the driver is notable in this picture. (JS)

95

B9R Coach Chassis

B9R was intended as a middleweight coach chassis, fitting between the lighter B7R and the heavier B13R. It was fitted with a French-built D9B engine, specified to meet Euro 5 emission levels and producing 380bhp. It was seen by operators as being a rather more refined version of the B12B with which it shared many components.

It was launched for the 2008 season with a Volvo demonstrator available from December 2007. It was initially available with Plaxton, Jonckheere and Sunsundegui coachwork, quickly followed by Caetano exclusively for National Express work. On more arduous work the B9R took over from the B7R. Stagecoach quickly purchased Plaxton-bodied examples for Scottish long distance services and for the Oxford-Cambridge route and National Express made this chassis, combined with a Caetano body, into their standard vehicle, thereby taking Volvo chassis to operators who had no previous experience of the marque. The Ministry of Defence moved from B7R to B9R again with Plaxton coachwork.

B9R sold alongside the B12B for a while but the requirements of Euro 5, which B12B did not satisfy, ended the duality. Like the B7R, B9R proved itself to be a very capable workhorse selling well in a depressed and very competitive market.

Stagecoach quickly built up a fleet of Plaxton-bodied B9R for express work where they were especially suitable for the 'long thin' routes into the Far North of Scotland. (PL)

The great majority of National Express B9R vehicles carried Caetano bodywork, but Selwyn's took two batches with Plaxton bodies before 'conforming'. They were used on the arduous trans-Pennine service from Liverpool to Leeds. One of the second batch is seen here entering Chorlton Street coach station in Manchester. (JAS)

Park's favoured Jonckheere coach work for their private hire fleet and took several deliveries with their distinctive registrations. After Park's purchased Trathens at Plymouth, their vehicles frequently inter-worked. LSK 501 is seen outside Paris. (KM)

Many operators established after the Second World War are now having significant anniversaries. Hughes at Llandudno – Alpine Travel – have got as far as a 40th Anniversary, no mean achievement in a seasonal operating environment. Perhaps ironically, Alpine specialise in taking customers on extended tours away from this holiday destination. Their Panther-bodied B9R was captured at Rhos-on-Sea, only just down the road. (DC)

Banstead Coaches had two more decades under their belt and celebrated with a new Plaxton-bodied B9R finished in a distinctive commemorative livery to celebrate their 60 years of service. The coach is seen posing at Goodwood. (DC)

97

Almost a fairy tale – two multi-coloured Lions greet a Panther at the head office, itself called John Bull House (and hence the JB registration of the new B9R), of Northamptonshire's Country Lion. This company has been a strong customer for the Volvo/Plaxton combination. (PL)

Looking quite regal, this Plaxton Elite-bodied B9R poses outside a suitable stately home. Grand UK are following the notion first explored by Wallace Arnold of creating a much more 'up-market' image of coach touring with high specification, luxurious vehicles. (PL)

This pair of B9R with Plaxton Elite coachwork delivered to Stott's at Oldham joined a Caetano-bodied B9R used for National Express work. The bright and cheerful Stott's livery contrasts markedly with that of the Northern Rail DMU passing on the viaduct – the coaches are a much more attractive proposition. (DC)

Sunsundegui provided the coachwork for a number of B9Rs. This example, operating in charter livery, belongs to Shaw at Carnforth – better known as The Travellers Choice. The company also operated a number of Caetano-bodied B9R on National Express work. (JAS)

Logans at Dunloy were early instigators of the Elite body style from Plaxton and took examples on B12BT and B13R as well as the B9R depicted here. The 2010 version of the Corporate Coaching livery suits the body style well. (MB)

Minsterley Motors in rural Shropshire has an astute management that enables them to regularly purchase new rolling stock – for both bus and coach operation. In March 2012 three new B9R/Plaxton joined the coaching fleet. The secret of success may lie in the corporate tour company livery of two of the coaches. (DC)

99

B11R Coach Chassis

The B11R chassis was introduced in 2013 as part of the preparation by Volvo for Euro 6. It was initially available in Euro 5 format, but now continues to the Euro 6 compliant range.

The chassis is designed to replace both the B9R and B13R. It is, therefore, available in both two- and three-axle configuration. It is fitted with a new 11-litre engine rated at either 370, 410 or 450bhp. The new engine is giving excellent fuel consumption figures – '...well North of 10mpg' when fitted with the Plaxton Elite*i* body according to Andrew Warrender of Alexander Dennis.

Less than 50 chassis sold in 2013, of which 14 have the new Plaxton Elite*i* coachwork – ten to Western Buses, two to New Adventure in South Wales and two to Matthews in Ireland. By 2015, however, the exceptional fuel consumption and high reliability of the chassis has led to a much larger operator base with many established Volvo operators taking their first examples. The chassis has been particularly successful in Ireland where fleet orders have gone into service with Jonckheere, Sunsundegui and Volvo bodies. The combination of the B11R and Jonckheere coachwork appears to have successfully filled the gap left by Van Hool exiting the body-on-chassis market.

The first B11R-chassied vehicle to be delivered in the British Isles was to Aircoach in Dublin. It was placed in service as a long term demonstration vehicle in mid 2012. For over 12 months the Caetano body remained unique. Subsequent B11R coaches delivered to Aircoach have carried Plaxton coachwork. (MB)

The combination of the B11R chassis and the Plaxton Elitei body has proved to be most successful for express service operations. The Stagecoach Megabus operation has been followed by Oxford Tube and Stagecoach services in Scotland. Plaxton re-entered the export market with deliveries of this combination to Polski Bus in Poland. (PL)

100

The first 'small operator' order for the B11R/Plaxton Elitei combination was from Matthews at Inniskeen in County Monaghan. The coach was exhibited at Bus and Coach Live in October 2013 before delivery to Ireland. It is seen here in the demonstration park. (RC)

The B11R has been successful in Ireland. McGinley at Gortahork in County Donegal has placed no fewer than eight Jonckheere-bodied examples into service – a major investment for a relatively small operator reflecting a high degree of confidence in the chassis/body combination. (MB)

New Adventure Travel is one of Cardiff's more significant operators with a very diverse fleet of buses and coaches. Two B11R arrived in May 2013 with the Plaxton Elitei coachwork – the first new Volvos purchased by this operator. En route to South Wales one was inspected by Andrew's at Tideswell in Derbyshire where this picture was taken. (DC)

B13R Coach Chassis

B13R was the successor chassis to the heavyweight end of the B12B customer range. It came with a 13-litre D13C engine giving either 420 or 460bhp. Although available in a two-axle configuration it has sold predominantly in tri-axle, 15m form. Indeed, only a single two-axle example has been delivered – to Hollinshead at Knypersley, Staffs.

Many examples have carried the Plaxton Elite bodywork, though it has also been sold with Jonckheere coachwork, notably to Lochs and Glens, and with Van Hool coachwork before that bodybuilder determined to cease to offer body-on-chassis combinations and to focus on integral vehicles of its own design. Volvo also offered their own coachwork on the chassis when the complete vehicle was sold as the 9700.

As with B12B it has been attractive to the operators of long distance express services – chiefly Stagecoach and Park's. The Scottish Citylink 'Citylink Gold' branded services use the Elite-bodied version, operated by Park's. With the Volvo body the chassis has also found favour with Irish operators of long distance services. Logan of Dunloy, an operator involved in the development of the Elite body, has taken several B13R examples, alongside B9R examples, for touring and private hire. A final flowering of the B13R is a significant batch of Jonckheere-bodied vehicles for Shaws at Carnforth delivered for the 2015 season. Externally B13R is virtually indistinguishable from B12B.

Despite the advent of the Euro 6 B11R, B13R continued to be delivered into 2015. This Jonckheere-bodied example of The Travellers Choice, Carnforth, in Trafalgar Tours contract livery, is in the Riverside Coach Park at Bath. (MJ)

An early customer for the B13RT chassis was Bluebird of Weymouth who use their Plaxton Elite-bodied example for extended holidays. (DC)

102

Chapter 3
From the Ailsa to the B5LH

The Ailsa was launched at the Scottish Motor Show in November 1973, and this represented the beginning of Volvo's involvement in the UK bus market. This prototype entered service as an Ailsa Bus Ltd demonstrator in April 1974 and is seen here depicted in Alexander (Midland) livery at Duntocher on the northern fringe of Glasgow. (JS)

The B5LH with Wright Gemini 3 bodywork is Volvo's answer to the need for a low emission, Euro 6-compliant double-deck bus suited to the conditions of 2015 and beyond. The bus is seen on the Volvo stand at Bus and Coach Live in October 2013. (RC)

103

The Ailsa Double-deck Underframe

The Ailsa underframe – it was noticeably not called a chassis – had its beginnings in the discontent being felt in the British operating industry with the first generation of rear-engined vehicles – Leyland's Atlantean, Daimler's Fleetline and Bristol's VRT. They were perceived to be nothing like as reliable as the front-engined vehicles that they were replacing, although this may, in part, have been due to the unwillingness of the industry to accept that the more complex rear-engined vehicles required a different maintenance regime. The Scottish Bus Group in particular was unhappy with the Fleetlines and Bristol VRTs that it had purchased and although it retained the Fleetlines it quickly disposed of the sole VRT intake.

The Ailsa Truck team were not slow to talk with the SBG engineers about just what they did want. Together they developed the specification for the Ailsa. The underframe itself was unique in dispensing with the traditional ladder frame and replacing it with a central spine and a peripheral frame, cranked over the wheels, to which bodybuilders could attach the body, thereby contributing to the structural strength of the whole vehicle. The engine was mounted at the centre front. The engine was the small, turbo charged TD70 Volvo engine that Jim McKelvie had introduced to the trucking world and which had astounded that fraternity with its power, durability and reliability. Everything else – gearbox, batteries and fuel tanks – were located as far back on the underframe as possible to even the weight distribution between the axles. The rear axle was to be of a drop-centre design to allow for a flat lower saloon floor, and, more importantly, for a lowbridge version of the vehicle to be built. Walter Alexander, as the predominant supplier of bodywork to the Scottish Bus Group, was involved from an early stage.

In March 1971 the Board of Ailsa Trucks approved the construction of two prototypes. To indicate a seriousness of purpose, a new company, Ailsa Bus Ltd, was founded in May of 1971, along with a company to provide spares and support for operators of Volvo buses and coaches in the UK and Ireland. Volvo took a 75% holding in these companies soon afterwards, in order to protect their name and reputation. Work began almost immediately on the Ailsa prototypes but it was 1973 before the first complete vehicle emerged from Alexanders. The Ailsa made its debut at the 1973 Motor Show in Glasgow. The two prototypes had grown to ten, all with the Alexander AV body and they were operated in some of the toughest environments – three with West Midlands PTE, three with Greater Glasgow, three with Tyne and Wear and one with West Yorkshire. The Tyne and Wear examples were fitted with Lockheed hydraulic brakes which proved to be troublesome and the batch was sold after only four years. The solitary Ailsa in the West Yorkshire fleet was sold to Derby. The West Midland and Glasgow vehicles enjoyed full working lives with their original operator.

The prototype vehicle went on extended loan to the SBG and resulted in an initial order for 40 underframes to be bodied by Alexanders and to be delivered to Alexander Fife. Although the engineers accepted the high revving,

How it all began. THS 273M was the first Ailsa demonstration vehicle. It was initially liveried in this faux-SBG scheme, but then passed to Midland Scottish who painted it into 'proper' Midland Scottish livery. It is seen here at Faifley near Glasgow on an early proving run, looking rather anonymous and clearly not in service. (JS)

turbocharged engine, mounted ahead of the front axle, the specification lacked a key factor that the SBG prized greatly – the ability to produce a lowheight vehicle. The problem was not so much the low bridges, of which there were not very many, but the low height of the entrance of SBG garages. (A classical case of the tail wagging the dog!) Despite this constraint, all of the group operators except Northern and Highland eventually purchased new Ailsas – and Highland took a number cascaded from Fife.

In 1977 a Mk II version of the underframe appeared with modifications in line with the experience gained from the first 330 or so vehicles in service. The major modification were to engine noise reduction and the options of Voith and Allison gearboxes. A Mk III version followed quite quickly in 1979 offering an uprated engine and a Volvo rear axle in place of the expensive and not very reliable Hamworthy rear axle. For some of the final deliveries to Strathclyde an air-over-leaf suspension was produced which gave a greatly improved ride.

A lowheight vehicle did, finally, emerge – as late as 1977 and for Derby rather than the SBG. The underframe – a lowered version of the standard product – was laid down in 1974 but the problems of a lowheight configuration took a long period of gestation to resolve. The major problems were the mid-ship mounted gearbox and the high driving position. In order for the gearbox to have adequate ground clearance within the lowered underframe it intruded into the middle of the offside of the lower saloon floor – an awkward arrangement. The driving position required the raising of the upper saloon floor above the driver's head, resulting in a 'blister' on the roof to accommodate the additional headroom. The mix of the AV deep upper-deck windows with the shallower AD lower-deck windows did not make for an aesthetically pleasing result. However, 'handsome is as handsome does' and the vehicle proved its worth with many years of service on the Derby Corporation route to Willington inherited from Tailby and George.

Ailsa Bus, and later Volvo, tried hard to open the overseas market to the Ailsa underframe. The prototype – THS 273M – was re-engineered to Hong Kong specification and shipped to Hong Kong to operate for China Motor Bus who were

One of the prototype vehicles went to Tyne and Wear PTE. It did not find favour and was sold in 1979, despite Tyne and Wear having an option for a further 50 underframes. After a varied career it joined many of its stable mates in Scotland. Rapson at Inverness operated the vehicle for many years. Shunning the destination equipment Rapson used a windscreen clip board – much tidier than the SBG habit of using paper sticky labels. (JS)

The first production Ailsas went to Fife Scottish who took 40 in 1975. In time they found their way to many other SBG operators and KSF 2N was with Highland Scottish when this picture was taken. Staxigoe is a small hamlet, once a major fishing village, north of Wick. (JS)

105

seeking a replacement for their front-engined Daimlers and Guys. Alas, Gardner-engined Dennis Jubilants and Leyland Victory won out (there was a good market for redundant Gardner bus engines in classical Chinese junks!) and only ten Ailsas operated in Hong Kong, including two of the three-axle variety 'Super Jumbos'. As a footnote it is worth recording that the Ailsa demonstrator was the first Alexander body to be supplied to Hong Kong – it succeeded where the Ailsa did not, as Alexander thereafter bodied many of the replacement vehicles for Kowloon Motor Bus, China Motor Bus and the upstart Citybus Bus Co, many of the later versions being on the Olympian chassis then produced by Volvo.

One demonstrator went to Singapore, with no follow-up order. The surprise was Indonesia that ended up taking over 300 examples in CKD form, with a rather larger number of Alexander body kits to provide for spares. This would have been a much larger order but for the intervention of Donald Stokes and Ron Ellis of Leyland with their contacts, resulting in Met-Sec-bodied Atlanteans taking part of a larger order. It must have been satisfying, in a slightly malicious way, for Volvo to observe that the Atlanteans fell apart much more rapidly than the Ailsas in the harsh operating conditions and erratic maintenance and, at that time, appalling roads in Jakarta, Medan and other Indonesian cities.

Beside double-deck vehicles, the Ailsa, in theory, offered the opportunity for both double and single-deck underframes. However, like the Derby lowheight vehicle, only one single-deck vehicle was destined to emerge as a new vehicle. A 36ft Marshall-bodied bus emerged in 1982. Originally intended for Tayside it was delivered to Strathclyde. Its working life was, however, curtailed by the Larkfield Depot fire of the same year in which it was destroyed.

Ailsas were involved in no less than three sets of trials or experiments. The first was with the National Bus Company when five Ailsas were supplied to Maidstone and District for comparative trials with Olympian, Metrobus and Dennis Dominator. No matter what the outcome, the cross holdings of the NBC and Leyland made it very unlikely that orders would follow for the Ailsa. Predictably, none did. The second was with a set of SBG trials conducted from their Milngavie deport, north of Glasgow. Once again, the competitors were the Olympian and the Dominator. The outcome of these trials were overwhelmed by privatisation. Finally, and most intriguingly, three new vehicles were supplied to London Transport in 1984 at a time when Leyland were in close collaboration with LT to produce the ill-fated Titan. Two of the LT Ailsa were ordinary enough and were supplied with dual-door bodies, but the third had a second, rear staircase, and an exit behind the rear axle. It has taken LT 30 years to adopt this layout more widely on the New Bus For London! No further new Ailsa entered service in London, although it was a popular machine when bought second-hand for work in London after deregulation.

There was only a self selected small group of operators of Ailsas. Not altogether surprisingly, the largest fleets were in Scotland – Tayside with over 160 examples was the largest operator, followed by Glasgow (in various guises) with over 150. The SBG took almost 190, but spread amongst its component companies, of which Fife took no fewer than 74. In England the PTE fleets of West Midlands and South Yorkshire predominated taking over 50 and 62 respectively. Merseyside took

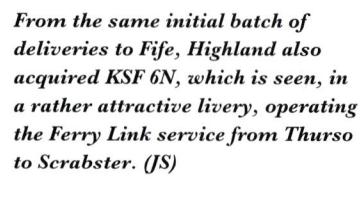

From the same initial batch of deliveries to Fife, Highland also acquired KSF 6N, which is seen, in a rather attractive livery, operating the Ferry Link service from Thurso to Scrabster. (JS)

This is one of 50 Ailsas delivered to West Midlands in 1976, an order which came as a result of the inability of Leyland to deliver Fleetlines on an acceptable time scale. West Midlands ordered a further 50 but the order was cancelled for political reasons. (DC)

15 and Derby 16, including the sole lowheight example. In Wales, Cardiff, a late convert, took 36. A small smattering of independents operated the Ailsa – the A1 co-operative in Ayrshire that ran services past Volvo's front door at Irvine, took eleven examples spread amongst its members – and Wilson of Stainforth took a single example.

Bodywork was constructed mainly by Walter Alexander (including all the export vehicles), a few by Marshalls – including the sole single-decker – whilst Northern Counties supplied some bodies for Derby and Tayside. The most interesting bodywork order was from South Yorkshire PTE who specified Van Hool McArdle bodies for their batch of 60 Ailsas, with two follow-on orders from the A1 co-operative.

The Ailsa proved to be an incredibly reliable vehicle and so loved by fleet engineers. But it was not sophisticated. For the passenger it was noisy and the ride from the leaf spring suspension was harsh. For the driver the cab was cramped. But, as the Indonesian examples especially illustrated, it could move a great many passengers reliably and effectively day-in day-out. With sales of over 1,000 it was not a failure for Ailsa Bus, but with the advent of a new generation of rear-engined double-deckers from Leyland, Dennis and Scania in the late 1970s, Volvo needed a new product. Delivery of the final batch for Strathclyde in 1984 marked the end of a fascinating example of entrepreneurial flair that had begun in Scotland some twelve years earlier.

Having taken three prototype vehicles, Greater Glasgow PTE took a further 15 in 1976. The traditional offside driver's door is well–illustrated here. Although drivers disliked the rather cramped cab, they did like the high driving position. Delivered in the PTE green and yellow livery it now carries the Strathclyde Buses orange. (DC)

From 1981 onwards deliveries to Strathclyde Buses – as the PTE bus operation had become – all carried Alexander's handsome R-type bodywork. This example was delivered in late 1982 and is seen in the south side of the city in the suburb of Pollokshields. The 59 route is an ex-tramway service. (DC)

107

South Yorkshire PTE was also frustrated by the inability of Leyland to deliver, and ordered Ailsas in consequence. The PTE selected unusual bodybuilders – Van Hool, who constructed the prototype in Belgium and the remainder of the order for 62 buses in Ireland at their Van Hool McArdle subsidiary. (RM)

A1 Services, based at Ardrossan, took eleven new Ailsas and also part-used examples, the most interesting being those from Maidstone and District that had been part of the NBC trials. This is an Ailsa bought new to Docherty in the A1 co-operative, waiting to return to Irvine at Kilmarnock bus station. The heavy duty front bumper is a unique feature. (RM)

Tayside operated the largest fleet of Ailsas, ahead of Strathclyde by a small margin – this is one of their third batch, delivered to Dundee in 1979. Tayside specified dual-door bodywork for all of its Ailsas and all but the final deliveries at the end of 1983 were by Alexander. The 1983 batch carried East Lancs bodies, seating no less than 84. (DC)

A1 also had the distinction of purchasing the only new Van Hool McArdle-bodied Ailsas other than those for South Yorkshire. Tom Hunter in the co-operative purchased two in 1977 as a follow-on from the South Yorkshire order. (DC)

Wilson at Stainforth near Doncaster – trading as Premier – was one of the very few independents to purchase an Ailsa. This vehicle was delivered in August 1976 and is seen here on its first day in service. The simple 2-step entrance is well displayed in this picture. (RM)

Derby was interested in the Ailsa from an early stage, especially as the platform for a low-height vehicle. Derby's General Manager collaborated with Ailsa Bus to achieve this goal. The manufacturer also wanted a lowheight vehicle for the SBG. However, the result was slow coming although Alexanders married parts from various designs to achieve the low height. The resulting bus remained unique and was not an especially elegant specimen. The contrast in height is illustrated here with the Derby lowheight alongside a normal height West Midlands example. Both are preserved by the 4738 Group. (JAS)

109

London remained an important target market, but produced an order for only three Ailsas, all bodied by Alexanders. Two were to conventional two-door layout, as seen with A101 SUU, left, on the 170 route heading for Aldwych. The third was remarkable for having twin staircases and a rear door as seen below. As such A103 SUU pre-dated the NBFL standing behind it in the lower photograph by almost 30 years! By good fortune two of the three have survived into preservation.

Volvo was more successful in London with the Olympian, inherited from Leyland, with the B7TL and the B9TL. (DC all)

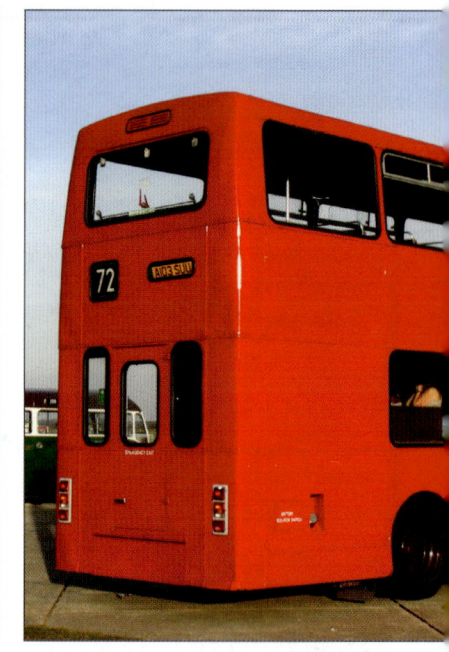

110

In 1982 Derby took delivery of a batch of Ailsas with normal-height Northern Counties bodies to join similar vehicles in the fleet. The neat detailing around the radiator grille and the driver door is noticeable. (DC)

An iconic view of one of the final batch of Ailsas to join the Strathclyde fleet. Air suspension gave the final version of the Ailsa a much pleasanter ride and along with other modifications gave a greatly improved passenger environment. Strathclyde's specification of a sliding door for the driver cabin is clearly visible. (DC)

111

Cardiff was a late convert to the Ailsa, taking their first delivery in 1984, but quickly amassed a fleet of over 36 new Northern Counties-bodied vehicles. They also added second-hand Alexander-bodied examples from Merseyside. This picture shows one of the Northern Counties vehicles new to Cardiff, built to a specification similar to that of Derby. By that time Ailsas were operating in three UK capital cities – Edinburgh, Cardiff and London. (DC)

Liverpool was an even later comer to the ranks of Ailsa operators. It was June 1984 before twelve Alexander-bodied examples arrived on Merseyside. After a relatively brief life with Merseyside PTE they passed to Cardiff. (DC)

Eastern Scottish, like its SBG counterparts, acquired many Ailsas, both new and second hand. They were used both for the Edinburgh 'local' services and for services into Fife and Midlothian. (JS)

112

Ailsas tended to move around! After ten years service South Yorkshire sold their VHMA-bodied examples. At that time de-regulation was hitting Scotland and many were snapped up by Scottish operators seeking to lower their capital investments, yet increasing their fleet size to ward off competition – as with the example on the left running for Eastern Scottish. Or, in the case of Stagecoach, to have a low cost vehicle to challenge existing operators using the original Magicbus formula of 'cheap, cheerful, frequent' – as illustrated on the right. NAK 418R is still in Hampshire Bus livery, as transferred to Glasgow, and is operating a tendered service to Torrance. (JS)

The example below was not all it appears to be. Although operating for West Midlands PTE, in West Midlands' livery, it is, in fact, a Strathclyde Buses vehicle. It was used as a demonstrator from May to August of 1981. It generated an order from West Midlands PTE for a further 50 Ailsas – an order that was subsequently cancelled for political reasons as already mentioned. It then passed to Merseyside PTE for five months, during which time it was 'sub-loaned' to South Yorkshire PTE. It was almost six months after the arrival of its fellow Strathclyde vehicles before it entered service in Glasgow. (DC)

113

An enthusiastic collector and operator of second-hand Ailsas was Black Prince at Morley, near Leeds. Black Prince amassed over 30 Ailsas from a wide variety of sources. They were painted in the distinctive red and gold livery, but with varying elements of both colours so that no two were identical. This is an ex-West Midlands example that was third or fourth hand by the time it reached Morley. Note the use of fleet number to match the registration, a not uncommon practice amongst smaller operators. (STA)

In the aftermath of de-regulation, many ten year old West Midlands Ailsas went to London Transport alongside a few South Yorkshire examples where they all worked from Potters Bar. The irony of this situation was not lost on Volvo personnel who had worked hard to place new Ailsas with LT. (DC)

Glasgow has one or two notorious low bridges which regularly decapitated double-deck vehicles. Ailsas were no exception, resulting in the creation of a single-deck Ailsa. This was painted in coach livery and used for the rural service, won under tender, to the north of Glasgow to Drymen and Balfron. A rather anonymous AS 2 hurries along towards Drymen in the Scottish rain. (JS)

Strathclyde Buses AS 1 was the only purpose-built single-deck Ailsa. Originally intended for delivery to Tayside it entered service with Strathclyde in 1983. The distinctive Marshall body was not unattractive. The bus had a relatively short career as it was destroyed by fire at Larkfield depot. (DC)

The most unlikely, yet also the most successful, market for Ailsas was in Indonesia. The underframes were supplied to Indonesia in CKD form and assembled by Volvo's local agent. The same was true of the Alexander bodies which were assembled by PT Ismac in Jakarta. These buses ran in Jakarta and other major cities and were frequently grossly overloaded and operated on indifferent road surfaces. Their rugged design meant that they outlived a batch of Atlanteans delivered at the same time. Over 300 underframes, including one tri-axled example, were supplied. Alexanders provided 20 'spare' body sets to account for accident damage and so on. (RC)

Hong Kong was a market that was dominated by British buses – with Gardner engines and Volvo tried very hard to enter this market. The original Ailsa, THS 273M, was rebuilt to Hong Kong standards and shipped to the Island. China Motor Bus was the only customer, taking six 2-axle and three-tri-axle 'Ailsa Jumbos' seating over 100 passengers. Hong Kong Tramways took an option for ten underframes, but never converted this to a firm order. One of the 'Ailsa Jumbos' awaits shipment to Hong Kong in China Motor Bus's then new blue livery. (DJ)

B59 Single-deck Chassis

This was a chassis that was far ahead of its time. The success of the B58 coach chassis in the UK led Ailsa Bus to import a B59 chassis as, 'roughly speaking' the B59 was a rear-engined counterpart to the B58, with low-floor city-bus configuration and with air suspension and automatic transmission as standard features as befitted its city-bus role. In 1972 this was a very sophisticated chassis. In order to make a comparison, it is worth noting that Scottish Bus Group were, at this time, specifying high-floor Leyland Leopard buses with leaf springing and manual gearboxes. Not surprisingly, UK operators, in contrast to their European counterparts, looked askance at this machine, partly because of its complexity, and partly on the grounds of the higher initial cost.

Chassis number 134 was exhibited at the 1972 Commercial Motor Show and at the 1973 Scottish Motor Show. It was never bodied in the UK. An earlier chassis was bodied by Marshalls in Cambridge with an attractive Camair B48D body and was licensed in November 1972. This bus served as a demonstrator for almost four years before being sold to Clan Coaches at Kyle of Lochalsh who, twelve months later, passed it to McDonald and Maclellan at Lochgilphead. Both of these operators used the bus for lengthy school journeys and found it extremely reliable in rather arduous operating circumstances, but far removed from inner cities. At some period, probably after its long sojourn in Scotland, the B59 went to South Wales where the centre door was removed. The vehicle then enjoyed an interesting period with Vauxhall Motors – purpose unknown – eventually passing to Catterall's at Southam in Warwickshire who removed all the useful parts and then sent it for scrap in mid-1986.

Seen here whilst on temporary demonstration duties at Preston, VEB 566L would probably be on hire to Preston Corporation, despite the evocative destination slipboard. (Ribble, as part of the National Bus Company had a major commitment to the Leyland National.) The level of the seat backs visible through the windows are evidence of the low-floor configuration. (ALS)

Seen in its attractive demonstration livery, having been licensed after the 1972 Motor Show, this view clearly shows the attractive lines of the Marshall bodywork. The fact that the body contributed largely to the structural integrity of the completed vehicle was seen by many potential customers as unacceptable. (JS)

Citybus Double-deck Chassis

Before the last Ailsa had been delivered, work was underway on its successor. In 1981 a B10M chassis – chassis 905 – was taken to Irvine and modified to take a bus body where it was reclassified as BD10-XB1. Not a great deal needed to be changed. B10M was an accepted chassis in the coaching field where it had developed a strong reputation. Like the Ailsa it was given a perimeter frame but the chassis was lowered on the suspension. The THD 100 engine was de-rated to 162bhp but the rest of the driveline was standard B10M with an automatic gearbox. The need for minimal changes kept development costs low and so allowed for low sales numbers initially.

The first example was bodied by Marshalls, as were the next three of nine pre-production prototypes. East Lancs bodied a further four – including chassis BD10-XB6 which was used as a Volvo demonstrator – and Alexanders the remaining chassis. Delivery of the first prototype was in March 1982 to Strathclyde PTE for development purposes. Fifteen months later three others were delivered to Derby City Transport – in June 1983 – with two other development chassis going to Nottingham later in the same year. The final pre-production chassis, with an East Lancs body, went to Singapore Bus services in February of 1984.

Thereafter Citybus production was at Irvine, using B10M kits that were shipped to Scotland for modification before passing to the bodybuilder. Irvine would order chassis in batches from Boras that were delivered with consecutive chassis numbers. Despite the low chassis frame of the B10M the lower saloon was still higher than on the equivalent rear-engined chassis. Low profile tyres helped, but did not resolve this problem so there was never any question of a lowheight Citybus being produced. The advantages of the Citybus were that it had a completely flat lower saloon floor, an enhanced seating capacity as there was no rear engine and a relatively low unladen weight. Air suspension meant that it was a much more pleasant vehicle than the Ailsa in which to ride.

Citybus hit the market at a difficult time. The Bus Grant in the UK that had enabled operators to claim up to 50% of the capital cost of new buses was being phased out. Deregulation and privatisation were the watchwords of the then Government. This period of uncertainty meant that there was little investment in new vehicles resulting in initial annual sales that were below those of the Ailsa in its final years. This period of change, however, opened up new markets for Volvo. Municipalities and PTEs that had 'bought local' or 'bought British' on principle, and ex-NBC companies that were no longer straight-jacketed into buying Leyland whatever its merits, were now concerned with 'the bottom line' issues such as reliability, operating costs, passenger retention and similar commercial matters that had featured less strongly before. These matters now began to take on significance. All of which gave Volvo opportunities that had not previously existed.

Initial sales of Citybus were steady rather than spectacular. Derby City Transport was an important early customer along with Tayside and the Scottish Bus Group. Nottingham became the first major customer to switch to Volvo with the Citybus in 1985. They were clearly pleased with the development chassis. In 1986 Northampton and Bournemouth became new converts.

In the late Summer of 1985 London Transport took delivery of a most interesting Citybus. It was fitted with what was called a Cumulo system. This system was designed by another Volvo company, Volvo Flygmotor AB. As a bus slowed the energy used in braking was transferred to an accumulator. This electrical energy was then used to start the vehicle until it reached about 20mph when the standard TDH 100 engine and driveline would cut in. The result was a bus that used appreciably less fuel as the engine was only idling for over 50% of the time. The vehicle that was almost totally silent in accelerating away from stops and passengers enjoyed a much quieter and smoother environment. This was a hybrid bus some 15 years before its time and still needed development work done – its performance, for example, was optimised at four stops per mile with clear running between stops. In London it was frequently held in traffic jams where the conventional engine cut in, so eliminating the benefit of lower fuel consumption. In 1985, however, fuel costs and exhaust emissions were not the major considerations that they are today so the Cumulo bus was quickly removed from service and returned to Volvo, who took all the Cumulo kit out and sold it to A1 Services as a conventional Citybus.

When Volvo reviewed production arrangements for the Citybus in 1986 it was decided to move production from Irvine to the bus factory at Boras who would supply a standard B10M chassis and leave bodybuilders to make any modifications for double-deck bodywork.

The pioneer Citybus entered service with Strathclyde PTE early in 1982 – badged as an Ailsa! This was one of ten pre-production prototypes. This Marshall-bodied example remained unique in Scotland as all other deliveries to Scottish operators carried Alexander bodies. (RC)

117

The Citybus basis of a B10M chassis meant that it had a low centre of gravity that enabled coach style seating to be fitted. Citybus could then be used for a variety of purposes, including express services. A number of operators fitted coach style seating to the standard Alexander body – eg Western National – but East Lancs produced a very stylish body that gave an impression that was more coach like than bus like and a number of operators took this option, using the Citybus for both bus and coach work – Plymouth Citybus, Lincoln and Bournemouth being good examples. Alexanders produced a very striking design for the SBG, the RDC, with a dramatic full glazed front, but only two of these bodies were produced on long wheelbase chassis. Both went initially to Fife Scottish, but then transferred to Western.

In 1986 the London market was opened as London Regional Transport introduced route tendering. This led to the largest order yet placed for Citybus when Grey-Green won a tender to operate the number 24 service across central London. 30 vehicles were ordered with Alexander bodies and became very high profile when they entered service in 1988 as the route passed the Houses of Parliament, Whitehall and Trafalgar Square. The buses used coach rated 245bhp engines, the most powerful in any buses in the UK.

The opening of the London market led to 1989 being the best year ever for the Citybus as London General, Boro'line Maidstone, London and Country all took substantial numbers into their fleets. Outside London, the newly privatised Trent took 24 and North Western 18 examples and Southdown took twelve. In Scotland, Strathclyde and Tayside continued to be loyal customers both taking substantial numbers of chassis.

Small batches of standard Alexander-bodied vehicles were produced for stock and distribution through coach dealers. This

Derby City Transport – destined to become a strong Citybus user – took another Marshall-bodied Citybus pre-production vehicle but not until mid-1983. They eventually amassed 25 of the marque. The 'advertising' suggests that this vehicle may have been used for demonstration purposes – but it is still badged as an Ailsa! (DC)

In mid-1987 Badgerline took delivery of twelve Citybus with Alexander bodies. This was part of an important order that marked the beginning of rebuilding fleets following privatisation. These Citybus, along with B10M buses and coaches supplied to Badgerline under the same contract, were all under a then unusual contract-maintenance arrangement. (DC)

118

made good sense for Volvo operating coach operators given the almost total commonality with the B10M coach chassis. In this way examples were supplied to Henry Crawford at Neilston near Glasgow, Dewhirst at Bradford, Finglands in Manchester, Filers in Ilfracombe as well as one that replaced an Ailsa with the Hanley Crouch Community Association. The A1 co-operative continued its allegiance to Volvo by buying a number of Citybus, including the ex-London Cumulo bus. Whippet of Fenstanton near Cambridge added three Northern Counties-bodied examples to its fleet in 1989 and 1990.

Northampton became a firm customer and received some of the last major orders for Citybus in 1991. Nottingham continued to purchase Citybus taking a batch as late as 1997 and a final, single example in 2002. This was not as difficult as might be supposed as Citybus was basically a B10M chassis supplied from the Boras factory.

Perhaps the oddest Citybuses – if they can be so designated – were a batch of Grey-Green B10M coaches that were shortened by the simple expedient of cutting the frames short at the rear and then mounting East Lancs bus bodies, resulting in a somewhat odd looking very short rear overhang.

Like the Ailsa, the Citybus offered the opportunity of commonality for double and single-deck chassis. Also like the Ailsa, little advantage was taken of this fact. The only single-deck Citybuses were a batch of five supplied to West Midlands in 1986 and fitted with the rather inelegant Alexander P type body.

Rather surprisingly given that the East Lancs coach seated examples could be likened to the Ribble 'Gay Hostess' coaches, no tri-axle Citybus with coach seating or even a coach body were ever built. The potential was noted in a road test by Noel Millier in Commercial Motor as early as December 1983 but nothing materialised from his observations.

The export market was approached at an early stage – one of the pre-production prototypes going to Singapore in 1984. In the same year Kowloon Motor Bus also took a single Alexander-bodied example. Neither produced a follow on order. Rather like the Ailsa, however, the export market flourished towards the end of production when Guide Friday took opentop examples for its Paris services operated by Cars Bridet/Cityrama. East Lancs bodied six chassis for delivery in the Spring of each of 1998 and 1999. Somewhat surprisingly, in 2002, however, the Swedish Government, as part of its aid programme, supplied 50 tri-axle Citybuses to Bangladesh, complete with Alexander 120 seat bodies. In that rough, tough and neglectful environment the Citybuses lasted over 10 years.

Most Citybuses remained with their original owners for their full life span, although with the advent of larger groups post-deregulation, they were sometimes moved within the group. The major exception was the batch supplied to Trent who determined that they were to become a wholly single-deck operator and sold their Citybuses to Plymouth. The solitary example supplied to Wrights at Wrexham passed to Rossendale Transport when Wrights withdrew from stage services. The remarkable longevity of the Citybus is attested to by the fact that at the time of writing there are still many examples giving good service to their owners.

Citybus was a vast improvement from the Ailsa from a passenger perspective – it was quieter and rode better and the ability to have a larger platform meant that passenger flow was both easier and more comfortable. The capacity for operators to fit coach seating meant that a number of express services, previously operated with bus seated vehicles, were substantially improved. For the driver this was... 'the bus that drivers have been waiting for'.. according to the Noel Millier road test who waxed lyrical about the driving position and the handling characteristics of the Marshall-bodied vehicle from Derby that he tested for almost 70 miles in North London traffic.

The demise of the Citybus was a result of Volvo's decision to purchase Leyland, giving them access to the high volume market developed for the Atlantean and Olympian.

Citybus had something of an identity problem. When first launched it took the Ailsa name, but that was quickly dropped. It then had a period as D10M – again emphasising the double-deck application of the chassis. Ultimately it was seen as B10M variant, by which time the peripheral frame had disappeared and the chassis was seen as being suitable for both single and double-deck coachwork.

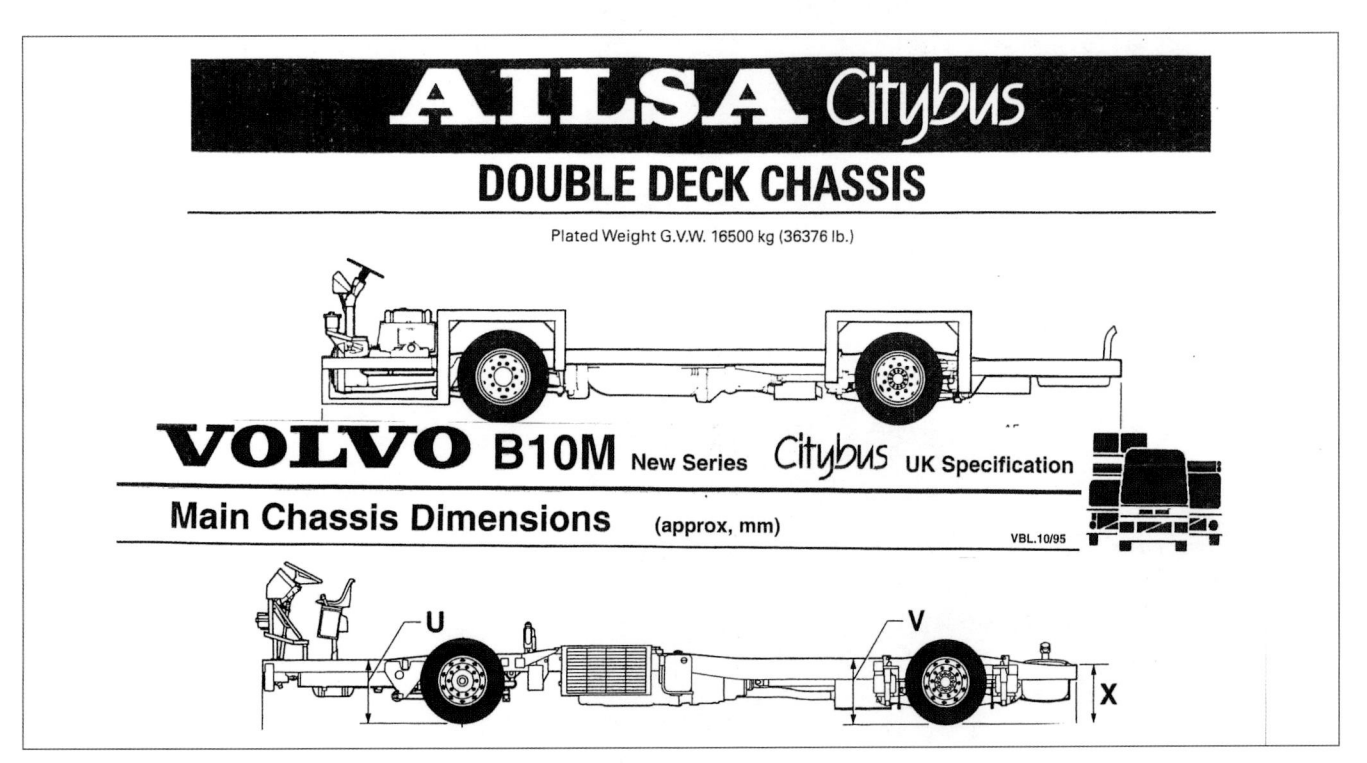

The Scottish Bus Group featured early in Citybus deliveries. It was an important market at a time when English purchases were depressed by privatisation. Fife, Scottish Omnibus and Western were the three companies taking deliveries. This is a coach-seated Fife vehicle in a later livery, on the lengthy route – dubbed 'Coastliner' – from Edinburgh, along the Fife Coast to St Andrews. The Alexander RV body was neat and workmanlike. (JS)

Greater Manchester took delivery of only a small number of Citybus, all with Northern Counties bodies. They featured a 'lifting platform' that enabled the disabled to use the bus with no assistance. GM Buses placed these vehicles in service on a single route and capitalised on the ability to carry wheelchair passengers at a time well before low floors and easy access became the norm. (JAS)

Fife also took delivery of two Citybus with Alexander RVC coachwork, originally in Citylink livery. Designed for the internal Scottish express services operated by the Scottish Bus Group these two vehicles remained unique on Citybus chassis. A well-loaded B175 FFS displays the striking front glazing of this design. (MB)

120

The impressive RVC vehicles were quickly transferred from Fife to Western Buses, where they were painted in that company's attractive express livery and used on the intense and arduous route from Glasgow to Ayr. When Citylink extended the 500 service – Edinburgh-Glasgow – to Ayr these vehicles were painted in a rather more garish early Scottish Citylink livery. Unfortunately they suffered from water ingress around the front glazing and were eventually rebodied as single-deck buses by East Lancs. (JS)

In all of the activity following privatisation, the Drawlane Group – antecedents of Arriva – purchased East Lancs-bodied Citybus for two of their fleets – London Country (South West) and North Western Road Car Co. This illustrates one of the North Western fleet in the rather striking livery devised for that company. (MB)

The East Lancs bodystyle made them suitable for semi-coach work when fitted out with a more luxurious interior. Two vehicles from a batch of five supplied in 1984 to Tayside were fitted out with coach seating making them suitable for private hire and express work – A289 TSN is the first of the pair. (MB)

121

City of Lincoln Transport was also attracted by the East Lancs body and took a small batch of four fitted with coach seating. The misalignment of the front windscreens from the side windows is very apparent in this view that has Lincoln Cathedral as a backdrop. (HP)

East Lancs also produced a more severe and spartan body style for purely bus work, illustrated by this ex-Volvo demonstrator that passed to the A1 co-operative whose services ran past the Volvo plant at Irvine. The smaller wheels fitted to the Citybus in order to give a lower entrance step are well illustrated here. (MB)

The real prize for Volvo, however, was the London market that had been freshly opened to tendering. Grey Green won a high-profile tender for the 24 route and acquired 30 Alexander RV/ Citybus to operate it. These were the first dual-doorway Alexander-bodied Citybus and were delivered in October 1988. Maidstone Borough Transport won a similar tender for the 188 route and used the same rolling stock with a striking blue and gold livery, and Boro'line fleetname. (HP)

122

It is interesting to see the various roles that the sales force for the Citybus thought it could fulfil. Much play is made of the flat floor enabling a rear exit behind the rear wheels and the Express Coach version could be seen as play for the market once occupied by the VRL coaches used by Ribble. The tri-axle, three door model is clearly ahead of its time - maybe this was the inspiration that led to the New Bus for London ??

- Citybus VERSATILITY

The Citybus is available in a wide range of lengths, even as a high-capacity six-wheeler grossing 23 tonnes. Whatever the length, there is more space for passengers to sit, stand and move than in any other bus of similar dimensions.

But sheer carrying capacity is not the only virtue of the Citybus underfloor-engine layout.

There's opportunity for efficient passenger flow as well.

With only wheelarches obstructing the floor, unrivalled scope is afforded for different interior layouts, different entrance arrangements, different staircase positions.

It is even possible to contemplate the return of rear entrances.

And the chassis can make an attractive low-floor single-decker too. The floor height is about 2½ft (750mm).

Enough flexibility is embodied in the design of the structure to accommodate all these variations. Special wheelbases and rear overhangs are within the scope.

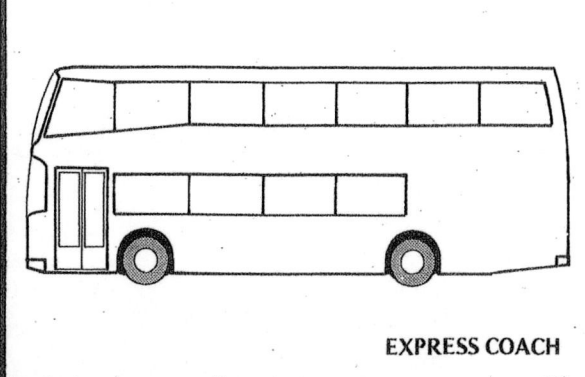

EXPRESS COACH

Trent took an early batch of twelve Citybus but once it had determined that it would become a single-deck only operation it quickly sold the Citybuses to Plymouth. Plymouth already had experience of these vehicles with a pair of coach-seated examples purchased new. Towards the end of its life F601 GVO had been relegated to schools duties. (KM)

Nottingham put their very distinctive design of bodywork on the Citybus chassis. This example is by Northern Counties but similar bodies were also produced by East Lancs. Having taken a pre-production example, Nottingham went on to purchase a further 22 Citybus. (RM)

The operator of the largest fleet of Citybus was Strathclyde Transport who purchased significant numbers in 1989 and 1990. Strathclyde was an early convert to easy access and had an Alexander-bodied Citybus fitted with a unique 'lifting platform' that enabled wheelchair access. It remained unique as the mechanism, mounted below the floor, was vulnerable to knocks and scrapes as well as road dirt. It is seen here being demonstrated at Larkfield Garage. (RC)

Only five examples of the single-deck Citybus were built, all for West Midlands, where they operated in the northern area around Wolverhampton. Initially painted in this attractive livery that suited the Alexander P-type body, they were soon repainted into a more conventional West Midlands Travel paint scheme. When withdrawn, all found a new home with Rapson, Highland CountryBus. (DC)

The `Cumilo Bus' did not find favour in London. It needed more development and the fuel saving imperative, so widespread today, barely existed, so there was no impetus to push the development forward. The unique traction package was removed by Volvo and the vehicle became a conventional Citybus. It was sold initially to the A1 co-operative and was later purchased by the avid collector of second-hand Volvo double-deck vehicles, Black Prince at Morley, near Leeds. (DC)

Northampton Corporation were late converts to the Citybus but over the three years 1990 to 1992 it came to form a sizeable proportion of their fleet. Indeed, the last batch of Citybus built went to this operator. The fleet passed to First Group who had problems in Northampton. Some Citybus were reallocated to Midland Red West, parts of which, in turn, were taken over by Rotala. Over 20 years old this example is still in First Group 'willow leaf' livery but with Diamond fleet names – Rotala's trading name in and around Redditch. (DC)

125

B57 Chassis

Volvo had a long history of producing rugged front-engined chassis that found a market in the developing world where they were sold under a variety of chassis designations. By the early 1980s this had been reduced to a single model, the B57.

In the UK the Scottish Bus Group, especially Alexander Northern, were interested in a low cost, front-engined chassis that would be more cost effective in operation than the Ford R-series vehicles that were used in a wide variety of applications, and which was less expensive and sophisticated than the Leyland National.

In order to meet the requirements of the SBG in 1981 Volvo imported a 10-metre B57 chassis from Sweden and lengthened the wheelbase to enable an 11-metre body to be fitted. Alexanders, as the coachbuilder of choice of the SBG, built a Y-type bus body to fit the chassis. Delivery was planned for late 1982 when the vehicle was scheduled to be put into comparative tests with Dennis and Ford vehicles. For a variety of reasons the project moved more slowly than planned and the completed vehicle was not delivered until March 1983. In the ensuing comparative tests the B57 performed very reliably but was heavier than its competitors and so used more fuel. It was also more expensive. Volvo were unhappy with the layout of the necessarily high-floor bodywork as it made entry for passengers quite difficult, but could not see a way of mitigating this with a front-engined configuration. As the SBG continued to purchase Ford R-series vehicles, the bus remained a one-off with Alexander Northern but led a full working life in rural Aberdeenshire and survived long enough to become part of the Stagecoach empire.

A further chassis was imported from Sweden in 1982. The 10-metre chassis was bodied by Wadham-Stringer as a means of producing a lowcost vehicle that might appeal to operators moving passengers over only a short distance. The vehicle was purchased by Ralph at Longford and used around Heathrow airport. It was not followed by any further

When XSA 5Y entered service with Northern Scottish in March of 1983, it was some three months later than planned. It spent almost all of its working life at Alford Depot and is seen above entering Aberdeen. (JS)

The bus lasted long enough with Northern Scottish to be taken into Stagecoach stock and receive Stagecoach stripes. (JS)

(Opposite page, foot) The first English operator of XSA 5Y was Alec Head of Lufton near Peterborough. The livery sits well on the attractive Y-type body. This was, allegedly, the last Y-type body built by Walter Alexander at Falkirk. (MB)

(Left) The Wadham-Stringer-bodied 10-metre example on the chassis, as used by Ralphs at Heathrow airport. The coachbuilders were based at Waterlooville, Hampshire. (MB)

examples. By 1989 it had passed to London Country (North East) Ltd. One other B57 chassis formed the basis of a horsebox for the Lambourn stable. It is likely that this chassis was imported directly by Lambourn and did not pass through the UK bus and truck operation.

An interesting development in 1993 was an agreement by Yeates to supply B57 vehicles to Bus Eireann. Not new vehicles, but twelve year old buses from Singapore that had been bodied in New Zealand by New Zealand Motor Bodies. After the maximum permitted twelve year life in Singapore these vehicles – suitably modified for a European climate – were used by Bus Eireann for school services for over ten years. The 335 B57 buses which entered service in Ireland under this deal enabled Bus Eireann to standardise and modernise its previously very 'rag, tag, and bobtail' school bus fleet.

Upper right: The vehicles that came to Bus Eireann from Singapore were from two distinct batches, both with New Zealand Motor Bodies, differentiated most notably by the front dome – one batch gently curved, the other flat, as illustrated. (MB)

Above left: The detail differences of the paint finish with Bus Eireann is also notable. Very few buses were finished to the high standard of VS 47, with black window surrounds. (MB)

Above right: Destined to become a school bus in a Celtic country – but this time in Wales – Owen at Rhiwlas operated XSA 5Y for a number of years on such services. (MB)

127

B7M Single-deck Chassis

There never was a B7M in the Volvo catalogue! The chassis plate gave the vehicle as B57 and used a number in the B57 series. B7M is, therefore, something of a myth and this interesting vehicle was destined to remain a one-off.

The chassis was built by the Experimental Department at Volvo Bus, Irvine, probably in late 1982 early 1983. The chassis used components from the standard Volvo list, a move that was designed to keep costs to a minimum – the frame, for example, was that used for the B7F, complete with front engine mounting brackets etc.

The resulting chassis layout was very similar to the then popular Bedford Y-type. The engine – a Volvo TD70 – was mounted vertically between the chassis frames and within the wheelbase. This meant, of course, that it was only suitable for high-floor applications.

B7M would have emerged as a chassis that was similar to the Bedford, but rather heavier and more expensive, though undoubtedly more durable and reliable. The market for such vehicles was already in decline and there was perceived to be no long term demand for such a configuration. It was decided, therefore, not to proceed to volume production.

The single chassis, numbered 8060, lay around for a while and was eventually bodied with a 53-seat bus body to a fairly basic specification by East Lancashire Coachbuilders. The completed vehicle was sold to Raisbeck Motors at Morpeth in Northumberland where it spent the whole of its working life. Ironically, in view of the decision not to proceed to volume production, Raisbeck found the vehicle to suit its purposes very well and were interested in purchasing further examples of the chassis.

South Lancs Travel of Atherton, Lancashire, considered using the vehicle after Raisbeck ceased to operate, but found the damage caused by the level of salt corrosion from Northumberland's roads not to warrant remedial work necessary to put it 'back on the road'.

Most unusually this vehicle spent its whole working life with one operator and on a single route – from Morpeth to Bedlington in Northumberland. Raisbeck eventually sold out to Arriva who had no further use for this unique specimen. This classic picture is possibly the only one of the B7M in service. (DC)

South Lancs Transport later purchased B212 JTY as part of a 'job lot' from Arriva where the bus had been out of service for over two years. The company explored the possibility of placing it back in service but the years of road salt in Northumberland had caused considerable chassis corrosion and the project never went forward. Not having been repainted whilst with Raisbeck and with some accident damage it looked decidedly shabby when it arrived in Lancashire. (MB)

B10M Single-deck Bus Chassis

Volvo had flirted with the idea of B58 as the basis for buses and had, as recorded on page 29, produced a few examples.

This rather tentative approach continued initially with B10M. The main purchaser was Hutchison at Overtown in Lanarkshire who continued to buy two or more B10M chassis each year and put bus bodies on them. In 1982 they stayed loyal to Duple, but 1984 saw two unique bodies – the Van Hool 'Local Bus' – and in 1986 they put Caetano Highwayman bodies on the chassis. In 1988 Plaxton made a foray into the bus market and having sent a demonstrator to Nottingham City Transport, a pair of Derwent-bodied vehicles duly arrived at Overtown. Two further examples to be delivered in Scotland in 1988 went to Strathclyde PTE who had won a rural bus tender and needed a dual-purpose pair of vehicles for this commitment. The Plaxton body was also purchased by Yorkshire Rider in 1990. Single examples, or pairs, went to several smaller operators. The Strathclyde and Yorkshire Rider orders marked the tentative beginnings of the fleet replacements programmes that were necessary after the doldrums of the deregulation and privatisation process.

The first major order post-privatisation came from Badgerline for a mix of B10M single-deck buses and coaches and Citybus double-deckers, all with Alexander bodywork.

The single-deck buses were bodied with the P-type body – not the most elegant Alexander product. The whole order was to be supplied under contract maintenance, an almost unique action at that time. The order also represented the beginning of what was to become a long-term relationship with what developed to become the First Group.

A small number of Alexander's rather more elegant Q type bodies, built in Belfast, were supplied to Trent and Timeline. A small batch from East Lancs was delivered in 1991.

B10M as a bus chassis was, however, really kick-started by the dismal performance of the early B6 chassis supplied to Stagecoach. Orders for over 100 B6 chassis were converted to B10M. The B10M with Alexander PS body became the standard single-deck vehicle for the growing and ambitious Stagecoach operation. Hundreds were delivered in the ubiquitous 'Stagecoach Stripes' and operated all over the country.

Duple and Plaxton retained a high-floor layout akin to coach production techniques. Van Hool lowered the floor line and had wider doors to make for easier access. Caetano, however, produced a very low-floor vehicle by bolting the body directly to the chassis frame and having only a gentle ramp to cover the rear axle. The Highwayman was, however, a little ahead of its time and only a small number were sold.

Hutchison at Overtown in Lanarkshire was an early and enthusiastic B10M bus user. Many, as this one, carried Duple bodies, but they also received B10Ms from Plaxton, Van Hool and Caetano – a most eclectic selection. This example is one of six delivered in mid-1987 – the first bus-bodied B10Ms on chassis to Mk II specification. (RC)

The first 'big group' order came from Badgerline who specified Alexander P-type bodywork. All of these vehicles were allocated to Weston super Mare and were under contract maintenance. This order marked the end of the drought of new vehicle orders by the major bus groups, and others quickly followed. (DC)

129

The technique used by Caetano was, however, picked up by Alexanders who, for 1990 delivery, won the order for a major renewal programme on B10M chassis from South Yorkshire Transport. The PS body was fitted directly to the chassis frame, had a wide entrance, two shallow steps and a flat saloon floor that allowed for 53 seats in a normal configuration, 48 in dual-purpose mode, and up to 65 as specified by Ulsterbus. Externally it was elegant and uncluttered. The same body/chassis combination also found favour in Singapore where several hundred examples were operated. The PS body on a B10M chassis became the iconic single-deck bus of the 1990s.

Up to 1994 bus chassis were all sourced from Sweden, but after that date they came predominantly from the Irvine factory with a minority of vehicles coming from the Boras plant. The last Swedish-built bus chassis went to Nottingham City and to Mainline, as South Yorkshire transport was known by 1996. Irvine continued to supply chassis for UK delivery including the large number that were delivered to Kelvin Central, the pair with East Lancashire Coachwork supplied to Delaine at Bourne in 1996 and the Burnley and Pendle deliveries in 1998.

The chassis was available with a DH101 engine rated at 260bhp for bus application, had air suspension as standard and could be specified with either a manual or automatic gearbox – the latter being by far the most common application.

By the beginning of the new millennium even the two shallow steps of the PS body were no longer acceptable. Low-floor was 'de rigueur'. The final B10M bus was delivered in 1994. The B10M bus chassis was to be followed by the B10L.

The Alexander Belfast-built Q-type body was specified by Trent for a small batch of five B10M used for express services. Unusually, these vehicles were based on coach chassis. The whole batch were sold to South Lancs Travel with whom M54 PRA is shown. (MB)

Burnley & Pendle were one of the relatively few operators who took the opportunity to have similar chassis for both single- and double-deck work, purchasing both B10M – for single-deck – and Citybus – for double-deck – operation. This basically Stagecoach specification vehicle, in the distinctive Burnley and Pendle livery, is on the 'main road' service from Burnley to Nelson. (HP)

130

Mainline in Sheffield adopted the B10M/Alexander PS as their standard single-deck vehicle and took several batches. One of the later deliveries is illustrated here at the Meadowhall Interchange, but the batches are indistinguishable from each other. (DC)

Disenchanted with the B6, Stagecoach converted its B6 orders into B10M, also with Alexander bodies. In an interesting move, the company re-equipped Cumberland Motor Services with almost an entire new fleet, many of which were B10Ms. In the original 'Stagecoach Stripes' this early delivery leaves the iconic bus station in Whitehaven. (HP)

Delivered over five years later, and one of the last deliveries to Stagecoach, other than the revised livery there is no difference between this vehicle and its earlier Cumberland counterpart.

The expectation that B10B would follow B10M into Stagecoach fleets was thwarted by a high degree of chicanery amongst those seeking that Group's business. (DC)

131

The coaching origins of the B10M chassis meant that it could easily be used for Express services and Stagecoach took full advantage of this. The illustration is of a vehicle prepared for the Manchester-Blackpool service, but in many parts of the Stagecoach empire the B10M/Alexander combination performed excellent inter-urban service, as for example on the Route 4 from Glasgow to Ayr. (DC)

It was possible to escape from the 'Stagecoach Stripes'. When the East Lancashire garages of Ribble passed to the Blazefield Group so did M232 TBV. Reviving memories of the one-time giant independent it is operating for Lancashire United as it performs less exotic duties on the route from Bolton to Clitheroe. (HP)

Not all Stagecoach B10Ms carried Alexander coachwork. A batch delivered to 'Southdown' were built by Northern Counties with 'Countybus' bodies. This example has been given a cherished Southdown registration. (STA)

When Northampton ordered a small batch of B10Ms they specified Duple coachwork to a high specification. Originally used on a country service gained on tender, the illustration shows that they were used on the Park-and-Ride service too. (DC)

Blackburn specified locally-built East Lancashire Coachbuilders bodies with dual-purpose seating for five B10Ms delivered late in 1991 – the first bus bodies on B10M from this manufacturer. This example is bound for the rather gloomy destination of 'Cemetery' and there is evidence of panel repair. (HP)

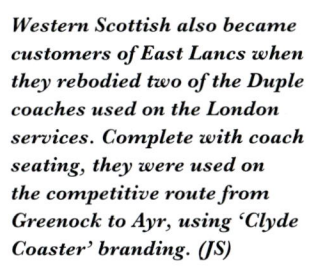

Western Scottish also became customers of East Lancs when they rebodied two of the Duple coaches used on the London services. Complete with coach seating, they were used on the competitive route from Greenock to Ayr, using 'Clyde Coaster' branding. (JS)

133

Delaine at Bourne has long favoured East Lancs coachwork. It was, therefore, no surprise when their order for B10M emerged from that factory. This view shows one of a pair en-route from Bourne to Peterborough. (PM)

The West of Scotland was home to a number of enterprising independents who took B10M chassis for bus work. Hutchison of Overtown was the major purchaser of new vehicles and his fleet included the rare Caetano Highwayman body. Vehicles were soon cascaded from that fleet, and many of them reappeared with other West of Scotland operators. (MB)

A well-known operator to take Hutchison vehicles was West Coast Motors at Campbeltown who operated services over the sparsely populated Mull of Kintyre. Most were contracted and this vehicle laying over clearly shows the Argyll and Bute sponsorship. It is parked-up at its outstation at Cairnbaan, next to the Crinan Canal, waiting to re-enter service, probably on a school run. (JS)

134

The unique pair of Van Hool 'Localbus'-bodied B10Ms delivered new to Hutchison led varied lives. This example, new as B947 ASU, passed to Henderson's at Hamilton then to Rhondda Bus – where it acquired the A15 RBL registration and later 'Stagecoach Stripes' – and then to GHA at Ruabon who reseated it to take 60 passengers. It has subsequently returned to the West of Scotland. Its twin was rebuilt after serious accident damage and is in preservation with Kenzie of Shepreth. (MB)

Plaxton Derwent bodies also appeared on the B10M bus chassis, and, almost inevitably, a pair went to Overtown. A similar ex-demonstrator, E31 BTO, initially used by Nottingham, went to nearby Graham's at Paisley where it joined an ex-Caetano Highwayman demonstrator. (RC)

West Midlands Travel was threatened by a low cost operator, Smiths of Alcester, south of Birmingham, who traded as Yourbus and took delivery of five Plaxton-bodied B10M from a stock batch in late 1990. Using this rather anonymous livery, Yourbus challenged the major operator on key arteries to the south of the city, one of the vehicles being seen on the Warwick Road corridor. Yourbus was later taken over and integrated into West Midlands Travel. (DC)

135

B6, B6LE and B6BLE
Single-deck Chassis

The B6 chassis took Volvo into an area in which it had not previously been represented – the midi-bus. That being so, it might have been expected that a company with Volvo's provenance would have taken care to ensure that the product was well developed before letting it loose on customers. Not so! The B6 was developed hastily, with an emphasis on using F6 truck parts to the maximum extent in order to keep development costs as low as possible.

The idea for the B6 originated in Austria at the Volvo owned Steyr truck plant near Vienna. There was a notion that the Low Countries in Europe wanted a relatively lightweight midi-bus chassis for both coach and bus application. In fact, the product suited the British market well. The 'bread vans' of immediate post-deregulation and privatisation were proving expensive to keep in service and were giving way to more sophisticated and purpose-built products. Dennis had introduced the Dart midi-bus and was having great success in London. B6 was intended to give Volvo a place in this market.

Some 20 chassis were produced initially by Steyr, of which nine came to the UK. By the time of the delivery of this small batch, Stagecoach had ordered over 100 of the model, with an option on further tranches. The small Steyr plant simply could not cope with this volume, so, with the encouragement of Stagecoach, production was moved to Irvine. This, of course, involved delay whilst Irvine geared up for production. It was late 1993 before production models were entering service.

Three chassis lengths were offered. A short B6-36, a medium length B6-45 and the full length B6-50. The engine was the TD63 of 5.48 litres, offering 180bhp and the chassis, unlike the competing Dennis Dart, had full air suspension.

Once production began at Irvine it grew quickly, with export orders featuring quite strongly. It was to Portugal, however, that many exports went, rather than the Low Countries, but Norway, Switzerland, New Zealand and France also featured. In 1994 Irvine produced over 400 B6 chassis, about half of which went to Stagecoach subsidiaries and the remainder to a wide variety of UK customers. Cambus and Bebbs at Llantwit Fardre were the only operators to choose the short B6-36 model with Marshall bodies. A very small number of B6-45 chassis received coach bodies – half a dozen by Caetano and four by Jonckheere – but as a coach chassis the B6 was not successful and further examples did not materialise in the UK. The remainder were the B6-50 model giving a 10m long vehicle.

In the UK Alexanders had been the lead bodybuilder. Marshalls only bodied the short vehicles mentioned above, using a design inherited from Carlyle Works when they took over that company's designs. Plaxtons and Northern Counties also built extensively on the chassis. Despite early success in sales the chassis was proving troublesome. The air suspension, that gave the B6 the edge over it's competitor, proved very problematical and the mechanical system was not always up to the rough and tough life in urban bus work and not always in a predictable manner. Ian Longworth who

The first B6 with Alexander Dash bodywork was delivered to Cumberland Motor Services. The chassis was built in Austria at the Steyr plant of Volvo, where the idea of a Volvo midi-bus originated. This is one of five prototype vehicles operated by Cumberland MS. The destination seems somewhat ambitious. The first tranche of 100 B6 for Stagecoach was widely distributed, but few companies in the group found them easy vehicles to work with. Indeed, so disappointed was the company with the early B6 that orders for a further 200 chassis were converted to B10M. (HP)

ran Timeline in Lancashire purchased two batches of B6 and he recalls that one batch would go out in the morning and happily operate all day long in a trouble-free manner, whilst the other batch rarely passed a day without one of them causing a problem. Not surprisingly, in 1995 sales dropped! Stagecoach made perhaps the most significant statement about B6, and altered all of its outstanding orders and options into the B10M – 200 vehicles.

Aware of the problems – and the warranty bills – Volvo produced a prototype B6LE in early 1995. Collaborating with Wrights who were developing a good reputation as innovative designers, especially for low-floor vehicles, the B6LE had smaller wheels, giving more opportunity for usable interior space. Volvo addressed the suspension problems with a slightly longer wheelbase. The TD 63 engine was retained with a power uprating to 210bhp available and a ZF automatic gearbox became standard.

Greater Manchester North was the lead customer for the B6LE-53 with Wright Crusader bodywork. Wright came to dominate the bodybuilder orders for B6LE with large deliveries to West Midlands. Alexanders continued to body the Stagecoach Group orders as well as Citybus orders from Hong Kong. Plaxton also bodied a large order for dual-door vehicles from Hong Kong, using the Pointer body. Other chassis were shipped to Hong Kong for local bodywork to be added. East Lancs bodied an order from Yorkshire Traction and, along with Northern Counties, also bodied vehicles going to a variety of small operators. The success of B6LE was mainly attributable to the skill of the body builders who could create almost as much interior space on the B6LE-53 chassis with its small wheels as on a B10L or B10B.

B6LE also revived the export business. Several batches went to Tunisia, with Greece, Switzerland, Spain and Sweden also featuring in the export destination list. One interesting development was a chassis that went to Northern Counties, but not for bus use. Although it received a more or less standard body shell, it was fitted out with all the communication equipment that was then available and operated as a major incident control centre. It was built to the specification of, and used by, Greater Manchester Fire Service.

In 1999 a further development of the chassis took place. The most significant development was the use of independent front suspension, allowing a much improved entrance area and the creation of easy wheelchair access – though most operators choose to allude to the easy access feature as creating a 'Buggy Bus'! The model was re-designated B6BLE. Orders from First Group and Arriva dominated the order book in the UK, along with Dublin Bus in Eire. All these deliveries had Wright bodywork. East Lancs continued to body for Yorkshire Traction and for Metropolitan in London and a small number of small operators – eg McConn at Rathcole, Morris at Bromyard – but no B6BLE was bodied by Alexanders.

Cambus was one of only two operators – the other was Bebb at Llantwit Fardre in South Wales - to take the short version of the B6 chassis. Bodywork in both cases was by Marshall of Cambridge using design inherited with the takeover of the Carlyle Group. Rail-link was an early example of the efforts to reduce the use of the car in Cambridge. (RC)

During the production of B6BLE Volvo decided to close the Irvine factory. As there was a good outstanding order book production was moved to the main chassis building plant at Boras in Sweden. Production at Boras proceeded for only two years. In 2000 the decision was made to cease production of the F6 mid-range truck. As there were many common parts with the B6BLE bus chassis it was decided that the economics of producing only for bus production 'did not add up' and B6BLE production stopped. The last B6BLE was delivered to Western National in April 2002.

In retrospect this was a bad decision. It left Volvo with no middleweight competitor to challenge Dennis, Optare and DAF. All of these builders have very successfully extended the weight and length of their vehicles to challenge Volvo's heavyweight product, the B7RLE. It forced operators to patronise a Volvo competitor if they wanted vehicles to operate in the middleweight range. It also forced them to dual-source and denied them the opportunity to have a single chassis and parts supplier.

It seemed strange at the time, and still does, that if Volvo's smaller competitors could successfully, economically and profitably source materials for a middleweight vehicle, that the might of the Volvo empire could not follow suit. In consequence Volvo deliberately took itself out of a significant market segment. Well, almost! Recognising that the decision to stop production of B6BLE had weakened the product line-up and was not helping the Volvo sales effort in the UK, Volvo entered into an agreement with DAF to sell the DAF SB120 chassis as a Volvo Merit. This rather feeble effort to replace the B6BLE was not successful – only Warrington Borough Transport bought into this blatant piece of badge engineering, taking just six examples in 2003 before sourcing directly from DAF. The arrangement was quickly dropped – and the DAF SB series has flourished.

B6 enjoyed popularity amongst Sheffield independents, with examples going to Yorkshire Travel, as shown left, Sheffield Omnibus, Andrews and Yorkshire Traction. Mainline also built up a sizeable fleet of later, low-floor, models. (DC)

This intermediate length B6-45 was purchased by Rhondda Transport and bodied by Plaxton as one of a batch of five. Eventually it arrived in the Stagecoach empire and passed to Cumberland MS. It is seen here at Dungeon Ghyll at the terminus of the route from Keswick along the Borrowdale Valley – a stark contrast to the environment in which it began life. (HP)

138

In the post-deregulation environment Timeline was established as a bus operating offshoot from Shearings. They took two batches of B6 with Alexander bodies. The performance of the two batches varied greatly, a situation not likely to endear any chassis to a fleet engineer. This is a vehicle from the first delivery of six vehicles in the autumn of 1984. (MB)

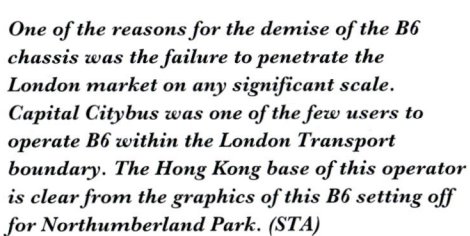

One of the reasons for the demise of the B6 chassis was the failure to penetrate the London market on any significant scale. Capital Citybus was one of the few users to operate B6 within the London Transport boundary. The Hong Kong base of this operator is clear from the graphics of this B6 setting off for Northumberland Park. (STA)

As early as mid-1995 Volvo, in conjunction with Wrights, had produced a prototype, low-floor B6LE. This vehicle went to London General and represented another serious attempt to enter the mainstream London market. It was destined to fail and this remained a single example in the capital city. The graphics on the side of the bus illustrate the importance attached at this time to a low-floor and easy entry, especially for the disabled and for buggies. (DC)

Volvo had considerably more success in the provinces where operators in Manchester, the West Midlands, Merseyside, Yorkshire and Glasgow were all B6LE and B6BLE users. This Northern Counties-bodied example operating for Greater Manchester Buses North displays the very short lived yellow livery. Note again the reference to 'low floor', 'green engine' and 'air suspension'. The bus operating industry was becoming very aware of environmental issues. (JAS)

West Midlands Travel had been a good customer for the B6 range. In 1996, after being rebranded Travel West Midlands, they took delivery of a substantial number with neat Wright bodywork. This example is seen in one of the more circuitous routes to Hall Green – a leafy south Birmingham suburb. (DC)

Despite their earlier experience with the B6 model, Stagecoach did come back for the more developed B6L and B6BLE models both for their UK operations and for Hong Kong. The latter operation taking considerable numbers of B6BLE. When they left the Hong Kong market Stagecoach repatriated many of their vehicles and put them into service in the UK. This example is operating in Coventry. (DC)

Arriva was a late convert to the B6BLE. They purchased small batches, possibly to keep their main single-deck supplier, DAF, on their toes. This is one of the later B6BLE vehicles with the chassis built at Irvine before production was moved to Boras in Sweden. Bodywork, as with the majority of B6BLE delivered in the UK, was by Wright. The vehicle was delivered to Arriva Herts and Essex in September 1999. (DC)

In 1999 Plaxton was still an independent company and set out to develop new products for the new Millennium. The 'Bus 2000' project, for a new single-deck body, used two Volvo B6BLE chassis – numbers 10155 and 10156. Plaxton, however, was taken over and became part of the Alexander-Dennis Group who already had established single-deck bus designs. The two chassis did, however, emerge in 2004 with 'Bus 2000' bodies. The one pictured here with Henry Cooper at Annitsford in Northumberland illustrates the influence the Plaxton design team had on later A-D single-deck designs. (DC)

Small, independent operators continued to purchase the B6BLE. Morris at Bromyard took a late example with East Lancs body to operate the rural services from its home town to Hereford and Worcester. This combination was a successful alternative to the Wright body favoured by the larger groups. (DC)

141

A new 2011-registered B6BLE, above, seems rather unlikely. However this Wright-bodied example began life in rather different circumstances. It was delivered in early 1996 to Aviation Defence at Heathrow with a three door configuration – two on the nearside and one on the offside. It was used exclusively airside and so never taxed to run on public roads. When it arrived in Ireland it was, therefore, a 'new' vehicle and hence acquired a 2011 registration. Now with only one door it has been extensively rebuilt. The vehicle is seen above in its original guise in British Midland livery operated by Silverwing Services and carrying N246 WRW as a nominal registration. The offside doorway is very clear, despite the grime. (MB both)

In Eire the purchase of new buses by small operators was rare, and outside of Dublin rarer still. This vehicle, seen left in the City, was delivered to McConn at Rathcoole in 2001 – late in the production life of the B6BLE and one of the last chassis produced at Irvine. The B39F bodywork is by East Lancs and the 'Dualway' livery tends to emphasise the small wheels of the later marques of the B6 range. (MB)

Dublin was home to a significant fleet of B6BLE. They tended to be used on more lightly loaded suburban routes but frequently penetrated the city centre. This view, below, is taken in O'Connell Street in the heart of the City. (RC)

142

Only the B6-45 chassis variant was used as a coach chassis. It was not a successful venture in the UK. Only nine Caetano-bodied vehicles were produced with a smaller number of Jonckheere-bodied examples. Stalwart Volvo operator, Ralph at Langley, used this Caetano-bodied example on hotel shuttle service at Heathrow. (DC)

Another Volvo stalwart to take a B6-45 coach was The Travellers Choice at Carnforth in Lancashire. This typically smartly turned out vehicle carried a Jonckheere body. The illustration is taken whilst the coach was negotiating roadworks in central Birmingham. (DC)

Another quality operator seeking an up-market midi-coach was Wray of Harrogate. Ideal for small party work the Caetano-bodied B6-45 was far superior to the Toyota Coaster and the various minibuses of the day. (DC)

143

B10L and B10LA Single-deck Chassis

Contrary to popular opinion, low-floor, low entrance vehicles were not developed for disabled entry, but in response to the need for quicker boarding times by fully mobile passengers. These passengers, it was thought, would board more quickly if they had to make only one step from the ground to the saloon floor. B10L was a response to this pressure, and came particularly once Mercedes-Benz had made inroads into the Scandinavian market – Volvo's 'home market' – with low-floor designs.

The design of the B10L chassis was entrusted to the ex-Leyland design team, capitalising on their expertise in independent front suspension. They had, however, to use the maximum number of standard Volvo parts, partly to keep cost to a minimum, but also to make engineering support both cheaper and easier. The chassis also had to accommodate the European need for 3-door layouts with an exit behind the rear axle.

The outcome was an impressive vehicle with disc brakes, (a first for Volvo on a bus application) and totally flat saloon floor. The engine was a variant of the TD 110 engine – the THD 104 – and gave either 240 or 285bhp which was coupled to automatic transmission. The chassis met Euro 2 specification. The Volvo subsidiary bodybuilder, Saffle, had developed a body specifically for the chassis. The prototype was delivered to the UK late in 1993 and, almost immediately, was put to work in Sheffield with Mainline. Alexanders were granted the rights to produce the Saffle design and Wrights also produced a design for the chassis.

It was not a very successful vehicle in terms of sales in the UK and Ireland, but it has to be remembered that the UK and Ireland were only part of the global market in which Volvo were involved. It was marketed as a high specification, heavy duty chassis with a design life of at least 15 years. In the period from 1995 to 1998 it sold mainly to Ulsterbus and to West Midlands Travel and, interestingly, to a small number of adventurous independents such as Timeline and C&M Travel. Dublin, Tayside (in common ownership to West Midlands) and Northampton Transport took small deliveries. Despite a show exhibit appearing in the livery of Fife Scottish, no examples were sold to the SBG subsidiaries, and the show vehicle became a Volvo demonstrator, registered N141 NDU.

No deliveries were made in 1998, but in 1999 there was a new variant. First Group had decided that it needed articulated buses and that it needed them 'now'. Volvo as a supplier to First Group, was anxious to gain this business and as B10L had been produced in articulated form for use in Europe, it was relatively easy to marry the 'pusher' traction package with a right hand drive front end. The result was the delivery in 1999 of 40 B10LA chassis, with Wright bodywork that went to a variety of First Group companies, mainly in the North of England and Scotland.

The final batch of two-axle vehicles consisted of ten with Wright dual-door bodywork for use in Dublin and Cork, delivered in mid-1999.

Alternative fuels to diesel were under discussion in the mid-1970s, following oil price rises and some concern about both the longevity and security of supplies. Compressed Natural Gas was seen as an alternative to oil and 14 B10L vehicles were delivered with engines modified to run on CNG. Of this batch six went to Northampton Transport, seven to West Midland and a single example to Dublin Bus. All the CNG-powered vehicles were bodied by Alexanders as the design of the body allowed for the installation of gas tanks. CNG-fuelled engine technology was not well developed and once the fears about oil supply had subsided the 'fashion' for alternative fuels passed and the vehicles were converted to run on diesel oil along with their fellows.

With sales of just under 400 over a period of five years, B10L, perhaps like its predecessor the B59 many years earlier, was rather ahead of its time for the UK market.

The first B10L demonstrator was registered in Lancashire – a tribute to the design team – and went for extended trials to Mainline in Sheffield. This was the only UK example to be bodied by Saffle and subsequent chassis had Alexander bodies, built under license to the Saffle design. Wright also developed a design for the chassis. The chassis was clearly focussed on the low-floor, high-specification, high-capacity market. (DC)

One of the interesting small operators to take delivery of the complex B10L was Timeline of Bolton - the Shearing spin-off. N304 WNF is seen on the 'main line' to Bury. (IL)

There was a time when diesel fuel was thought to have only a relatively short period of availability. Compressed Natural Gas was seen as an alternative fuel. Several operators and manufacturers experimented with CNG, but it was a short lived fashion and all vehicles reverted to diesel fuel. The B10L was well placed for these experiments as the strength of the body structure allowed the gas tanks to be roof mounted. P504 MVV is one of a small batch that went to Northampton. (DC)

A major operator to take delivery of gas powered B10L was West Midlands Travel. This posed shot shows, on careful examination, the 'blister' on the roof to accommodate the air tanks. CNG vehicles were always a tiny minority in the fleet, and as they required special attention they were unpopular with maintenance staff. Drivers and passengers noticed no difference. (DC)

145

The B10L was originally marketed as the Ultra - reflecting the ultra low floor for a vehicle of that time. This is reflected in the registration for this ex-demonstrator, M10 ULF. After 12 months as a demonstration vehicle it was sold to Strathclyde Buses where it joined other demonstration vehicles and also a small batch of seven vehicles built new for that operator. It is seen here after First Group had taken control of Strathclyde Buses and repainted it into what was then the standard pre-Barbie livery. (DC)

In Northern Ireland Citybus and Ulsterbus were amongst the most enthusiastic purchasers of the B10L. This Citybus example entered service in March 1997. The slightly different arrangement of the rear radiator on the production vehicles is apparent here, in contrast to M10 ULF above. (DC)

146

West Midlands Travel was the largest purchaser of B10L, with examples being delivered not only to the parent West Midlands Travel company but also to the Smith, Shennington subsidiary. Tayside Travel (also part of the National Express Group) purchased B10L but with Wright bodywork. P10 KOX in full West Midlands livery is seen in a leafy Birmingham suburb. (DC)

This Belfast Citybus was showing the ease of entry with its low-floor access when photographed at a Bus and Coach event. (DC)

The articulated version of the B10L chassis – the B10LA – was sold only to First Group, who bodied the articulated vehicles with Wright coachwork. During 1999 examples were delivered to First Group companies in Manchester, Leeds and, as depicted here, Glasgow. The high seating capacity of 55, plus an equal number of standees, enabled them to move large crowds very quickly. (DC)

B10B and B10BLE Single-deck Chassis

B10B was intended to be a Lynx replacement using the maximum number of B10M parts. This, inevitably, resulted in some compromises, one of the more important being that it had a higher floor than the Lynx which had to rise over the straight rear axle. The engine was the THD engine, with a power output of 245bhp which was more than adequate for urban and inter-urban services, and which met the forthcoming Euro 2 emission standards.

The B10B was launched in June 1992 with an Alexander body named Strider after the launch customer, Yorkshire Rider. The first completed vehicles entered service in early 1993. The early examples also carried bodies by Northern Counties – who produced the first Volvo demonstrator – and by Wrights.

Two important orders came for delivery in 1993. 13 Northern Counties-bodied vehicles, with dual-door bodies, were ordered by London Transport. This was the first single-deck order for London Transport and hopes were high of repeat business. This was not to be as LT found the 36ft vehicles difficult to handle. The other important order was for a batch for Trent that came very early in the life of B10B. 20 years later many of the Trent batch were still in active service.

Merseyside and West Midlands quickly became established customers using the attractive Wright bodywork. Plaxton bodied a number of B10B for City of Oxford, including a dual-door batch in 1997, using their new Verde body.

It quickly became apparent that the higher floor of B10B was limiting sales. B10L was supposed to take the full low-floor market but, with a few exceptions, had failed to do so. The front frame of the B10L was, therefore, added to the B10B resulting in a vehicle that gave a low entrance to satisfy the demand for such a configuration, and yet retained the relatively simple rear layout of the B10B. The outcome was the B10BLE. This was a great success. Merseybus and West Midlands ordered large numbers – over 300 in the case of West Midlands (who later altered some of the order to B10L!)

The B10BLE also proved attractive to the emerging mega-groups who were renewing fleets that had been becoming older whilst deregulation and privatisation took place. Both First Group and Arriva took many examples. With First Group the B10BLE/Wright combination became very popular, with the Alexander body being a minority choice for the Group. Mainline and Ulsterbus/Citybus took substantial deliveries at regular intervals and the Go-Ahead group also became a regular customer. The Blazefield Group, with many inter-urban services, tended to take high specification interiors.

Stagecoach, with a vast number of B10M buses, seemed likely to order B10BLE as a successor to B10M and, indeed, did so, but for only ten Northern Counties-bodied examples that went to Manchester. An order for 350 was never confirmed. The intrigue and double-dealing that lay behind this decision is amazing and showed competition for business at its worst and illustrated graphically how necessary corporate controls are in large organisations. It led not only to Volvo losing the order to MAN, but for MAN and Voith and Stagecoach to be

A real 'Clapham Omnibus'! A potential breakthrough into London single-deck bus provision came with an order for 13 Northern Counties-bodied B10B. Ironically, in view of recent developments, the 36ft long vehicles were determined to be too restricted for use in London and no further orders were placed by London Transport for B10B. (DC)

Another important order placed shortly after the launch of the chassis came from Trent MS, again with Northern Counties bodywork. M38 PRA is depicted here with new Rainbow Route destination display. (DC)

After over 20 years in service several vehicle from the same order are still in use, albeit on contract services rather than on the front line. Still looking very smart in University of Derby contract livery, it is parked up in Buxton. (DC)

148

left with a total mess that cost them all a great deal of money over a ten year period.

In Ireland Dublin Bus and Bus Eireann took examples and in the UK a group of doughty independents on Merseyside such as CMT at Aintree, Gemsam, Liverbus and Fareway invested heavily in new B10Bs. In 1999 a batch of 20 stock vehicles were supplied to a wide variety of small operators as diverse as Kennealy in Waterford, Duff of Sutton in the Forest, Rapsons in Inverness, White at Bridge of Walls and Morris at Bromyard. Inevitably, Hutchisons at Overtown took a pair and their neighbours Whitelaws at Stonehouse also took examples. Small operators continued to feature in deliveries, aided no doubt by the proximity of pretty well all UK bus operators to a Volvo service centre.

The last deliveries of B10BLE were, perhaps fittingly, to Yorkshire Coastliner who took two Wright-bodied vehicles with a very high specification interior. Over 1,550 chassis had been supplied over the nine year period from 1993 to 2002.

The launch customer for B10B was Yorkshire Rider who selected a new Alexander body named Strider. This vehicle, one of a batch of 20, was destined for Huddersfield. (JAS)

The first major order for the B10B/Wright combination came from Greater Manchester Buses North – who clearly regarded it as a Superbus. At this time, when low-floor was a novelty, there was a keenness to extol the virtues of bus travel as exhibited by the branding on the nearside of this vehicle. (DC)

149

Scottish independent operators were quick to purchase B10B. Whitelaw's at Stonehouse, who operate over a wide area of South Lanarkshire, took five with Northern Counties bodies and three with Alexander bodies. Shown here is one of the latter, delivered in January 1984. (MB)

As a keen user of the B10M bus chassis it was almost inevitable that Hutchison's would take a pair of early B10B fitted with Northern Counties bodies. The company also took B10BLE chassis with Alexander bodies. (MB)

A potential breakthrough order came from Eastern Scottish who placed 13 Alexander-bodied examples in service. The company also took the first Wright-bodied example that was used as a static demonstrator before delivery. (MB)

Plaxton were very quick off the mark to offer their new Verde bus body on the B10B and in mid-1994 Cleveland Transit took a batch of eight vehicles to this combination – one also favoured by Nottingham City Transport and City of Oxford. (JS)

A major customer for both the B10B and the B10BLE was West Midlands who favoured Wright bodywork. This B10B example is seen in central Birmingham in pre-National Travel livery. (DC)

By contrast, a later B10BLE/Wright vehicle in the Travel Dundee operation of National Express is in full company livery. It is not uncommon for vehicles to move between Dundee and Birmingham. (DC)

151

Stagecoach stripes did adorn B10B, but only when Stagecoach acquired other operators. This example was new to Greater Manchester Buses South in the Spring of 1997. (DC)

B10BLE continued the long-running relationship between First Group and Volvo. Many Wright-bodied B10BLE were delivered to a wide variety of the Group companies. This example is with First in Sheffield, the successor to Mainline who had been staunch supporters of Volvo products.(DJ)

Seamarks at Luton was a small, high quality operator. They took a single B10BLE with Wright Renown bodywork in a rather distinctive and attractive livery to operate their one local service. It is noteworthy that the company also took a single example of the C10M coach. (DJ)

B10BLE sold to a number of small, independent operators who needed reliable, heavyweight chassis. DRM of Bromyard ran regular services from its home town to Hereford and Worcester using this Alexander-bodied example. The fitting of emergency lights is an interesting addition to the normal specification. (DC)

Not surprisingly, deliveries of B10B to Ulsterbus carried Ulster-built Wright bodywork. Translink, as it later became, branded urban operations in Belfast as Metro and it is in this livery that BCZ 2805 is depicted. (DC)

Hopley of Mount Hawke in Cornwall operated this Wright-bodied B10BLE fitted, unusually, with 3+2 seating giving a capacity for 60 seated passengers. It is seen here in Truro bus station. After a relatively brief life in Cornwall it joined the well known fleet of Delaine at Bourne in Lincolnshire. Here it joined another part used example from Sovereign, Harrow of almost identical vintage. (ADS)

At the other end of the United Kingdom V258 DPS operates for White, Bridge of Walls in the Shetland Islands. (MB)

Most of the component companies of the Blazefield Group took delivery of significant numbers of B10B and B10BLE, most with Wright bodywork. Distinctive liveries were a feature of this Group and Keighley and District was no exception. The location is Skipton. (DC)

154

The great majority of B10BLE deliveries carried Wright bodywork, as illustrated by this Brighton and Hove example delivered in early 1998. Fellow Go-Ahead companies in the North East of England received similar vehicles. (DJ)

It was unusual for an Irish independent to buy new service buses. However, Halpenny at Blackrock had sufficient confidence to take two B10B with Wright bodywork in mid-1996. This was the first one to be delivered. The glazing on the front nearside window appears to have suffered a 'malfunction'. (MB)

At deregulation Merseyside Transport developed several new brands. Amongst them was Lancashire Travel, designed to attack the market north of Manchester. New vehicles were used to establish these brands. This Wright-bodied B10B exemplifies the efforts made to establish these new operations as being of high quality. Quite quickly these ventures, including a foray in to London, were either withdrawn or sold-on. (DC)

155

B7L and B7LA Chassis

The B7L was designed as a replacement for the B10B and the B10L single-deck chassis and as an Olympian double-deck replacement. It was introduced for 2000 deliveries. It was a highly sophisticated, high specification product. The engine was offset to the UK nearside with various components housed in what became called 'the wardrobe' that intruded through the whole of the saloon to roof level. The design gave a much larger low-floor area than in any previous chassis. In an otherwise very passenger friendly vehicle it gave a rather claustrophobic feel to the rear of the saloon where there was only a small window above a double seat.

Its origins in a design for mainland Europe made it ideal for articulated vehicles, with the pusher unit at the rear and a very large low-floor area. As a successor to the B10L it inherited the need of First Group for an articulated bus and the first deliveries were all B7LA chassis to the articulated specification laid down by First Group. First Group were also the major purchaser of the two-axle variant. Indeed, of the almost 500 sold in the UK all but a handful went to First Group companies. They were sold with a full maintenance package, so that the maintenance staff employed by First Group transferred to Volvo. This was an interesting 'first' (pardon the pun) in the UK bus industry whereby the vehicle supplier was responsible for keeping it on the road. Volvo had for a long time made much of the parallel with the aircraft industry where an expensive asset has to be available for high utilisation to justify the initial high investment. In the aircraft industry this support is often provided either by the airframe manufacturer or the engine manufacturer. Although this practice is widespread in the airline industry it failed to gain traction in the bus industry on any scale in the UK and the B7L arrangements with First Group remain unique.

At the time that B7L was introduced Alexander were in a state of flux as the company had been put up for sale. Volvo relied quite heavily on Alexander as body building partners. In order to potentially safeguard their position two chassis were bodied by Hispano in Spain – one articulated and one two-axle vehicle. In the event Alexander was sold to Mayflower Engineering and no further Hispano vehicles were imported. It was not surprising, therefore, that the great majority of B7L were bodied by Wright.

By the late 1990s the sales of the Olympian were falling as customers demanded a low-floor vehicle. Volvo in Sweden saw B7L as solving the problem. A pre-production chassis was sent to Plaxtons to be bodied with a prototype of their new low-floor body, the President. The result was a 36ft long, dual-door double-deck vehicle, exhibited at the Coach and Bus Show in 1997. Designed to compete with the new Dennis Trident it was a resounding flop! It took Volvo almost three years to produce a competitor to the Trident in the shape of B7TL, during which time Volvo lost their ascendancy in the double-deck market that they had bought rather expensively with the purchase of Leyland a decade earlier.

This view, taken on a wet day in Wigan at the old Northern Counties premises, by then owned by Plaxton, shows the length of the bus. Although the chassis failed to find orders, the President body was very successful and influenced later designs. (PL)

A prototype chassis and a prototype body – B7L with Plaxton President body. It is seen here on demonstration to Lothian Transport in Edinburgh, one of the few operators to seek a demonstration. Intended as an Olympian replacement the double-deck B7L failed to produce even a single order. It was back to the drawing board for Volvo. (SP)

The show vehicle was never registered though it did go on demonstration to a few brave operators. London – the target market – rejected it totally. It then lay unloved and neglected for many years before passing to Manchester College who used it to demonstrate the independent front suspension. Remarkably, in 2013 it was still virtually intact in a Winsford dealer's yard.

London did, however, take three examples of the B7L. A single two-axle vehicle and two articulated Wright-bodied examples were supplied to Centre West in 2008. B7L was a very adaptable chassis and was available in a tri-axle rigid design. This format was bodied by East Lancashire Coachbuilders who supplied 20 left hand drive models to Denmark, where they operated in Copenhagen.

Always willing to try to improve productivity, First Group then followed suit and took delivery of ten tri-axle, 95-seat, double-deckers for their First Glasgow subsidiary at the end of 2002.

The tri-axle chassis also found favour as the basis for an open top tour bus. East Lancs-bodied three to part open top specification for use in Luxembourg. The major surprise, however, was a large number produced with Ayats bodies that were purchased by Guide Friday, Ensign and Bath Bus Co for open top tours. Almost 20 of these interesting vehicles were delivered in the 2005/2006 period. It is worth noting that at this time Ayats were having considerable success elsewhere in Europe with their open top design on B7L chassis.

Not content with innovation on maintenance for the B7L, and on tri-axle double-deckers, First Group took another innovative step in collaboration with Wright and Volvo and produced the StreetCar. This was a basically a standard B7LA chassis, modified to give a slightly more central driving position that was isolated from the saloon. It was then fitted with a 'tram like' full fronted, dual entrance body produced by Wrights. This was a response to the urge by many local authorities to return to the perceived 'golden age' of the tram, yet who could not afford new tram systems or even a guided busway.

First Group introduced the StreetCar in co-operation with local authorities who were required to create bus lanes and to improve street furniture in such a way that travel by public transport was seen to be attractive and speedy – in fact, just like a tram. The concept was brilliant.

The execution was not always so good. First introduced new on-board ticketing systems to go with StreetCar and this was not always very effective, so speed of boarding was lost. Local authorities, having promised major changes in infrastructure, frequently failed to deliver, so journey times were not as speedy as planned. The first operation of StreetCars was in York in 2006. Teething troubles apart, the applications did settle down to give a much improved service to passengers. It took some time, however, for some infrastructure improvements to take place and the last Street Cars did not enter service until 2008, in Swansea.

The first production deliveries of B7L were single-deck articulated versions (B7LA) to First Group. Delivered to Yorkshire Rider in 2000 this example is at work in Bradford. Similar vehicles went to Aberdeen and Hampshire. With a low floor throughout both sections of the bus they were extremely good at moving large crowds very quickly. (DC)

Dublin Bus also took the articulated version of the B7L. This Wright-bodied example, equipped with air conditioning, loads in O'Connell Street. The attractive Dublin Bus livery tends to emphasise the length of these vehicles. (RC)

157

With a Wright body and the attractive 'Willow leaf' livery of First Bus this offside view of the B7L is almost indistinguishable from other Wright-bodied single-deck vehicles. This example was used for demonstration purposes before delivery to Mainline in Sheffield – hence the Y900 FML registration to match the fleet number. (JAS)

These rear views, however, shows very clearly the distinctive 'wardrobe' for the engine and ancillary fittings that led to only a small rear window. The vehicle is, again, First Mainline No. 900. (JAS)

158

A solitary, rigid, B7L went to London, operated by Go-Ahead subsidiary London General. Like other attempts by Volvo to gain entry to the London single-deck market it was destined to fail. Two articulated examples, delivered late in the life cycle of the B7L also remained as one offs. (TQ)

Significantly, Alexanders did not body a single B7L. At that time they were in a state of confusion and Wright took the bulk of orders. Volvo safeguarded their supply chain by having two B7L bodied by Hispano – a rigid vehicle, as illustrated, and an articulated chassis. The rigid spent some time on demonstration work and ended up in the fleet of McGill's at Barrhead near Paisley. The artic spent most of its time at Manchester Airport and is now an exhibit in the airport display area. (DC)

The versatility of the chassis is shown by the application of a double-deck body on a tri-axle configuration. First Glasgow took ten of these high capacity vehicles – they seated 95 – and used them on the intense service to East Kilbride. The long rear overhang does, however, emphasis the European origin of the chassis. Where on this example there is an emergency exit behind the rear axle, in Copenhagen, where 40 vehicles of this design were operated, this was a standard, third, exit door. (DC)

159

The versatility of the B7L chassis was demonstrated further by its use as the base for a sight-seeing bus. Ayats had already bodied a number of examples for use in Europe and a right hand drive version was relatively easy to engineer. Arriva purchased eight examples in 2005 for the Original London Tour. Other examples went to Bath Bus and Guide Friday. (TQ)

StreetCar, based on the B7L, was very innovative. It was designed to allow local authorities to introduce a 'tram like' experience without the expense of trams! The driver was isolated from the passengers and the StreetCar was supposed to run in an improved environment including dedicated stops and a having a high priority at junctions etc. The first major application of the concept was in York on the cross city service No.4. (DC)

The revised position of the front axle is clearly shown here and the wheelguards allow a very streamlined appearance. In practical application the idea was less than 100% successful. StreetCar had to battle with traffic like an ordinary bus. It was not helped in York by the expensive need for a conductor and a new on-board ticketing system (DC)

The StreetCars deployed in York have subsequently been withdrawn and redeployed on a new express Hyperlink service from Bradford to Leeds. (JAS)

B7RLE Single-deck Chassis

B7L was only a very modest success. The development of that chassis to become the B7RLE has resulted in one of the more successful chassis produced by Volvo since the B10M.

The chassis has won approval and orders from a very wide variety of operators, including all of the major groups – even Stagecoach, closely tied to the AD group, have purchased new B7RLE/Wright for the Cambridge Busway. Notably, it became the standard heavyweight single-deck chassis for First Group from 2005 onwards with several hundred chassis delivered to this operator. The chassis has also had a strong following amongst small operators and they featured heavily in early deliveries in 2003 – Minsterly Motors, Longstaff, Hutchison, KMP, Perryman, Halpenny and Whitelaw all featuring. West Midlands and Lothian have also been loyal users of the chassis – the latter's Chief Engineer when taking delivery of a 2013 order for 15 vehicles publicly wished that he had had 100. Bus Eireann and Trent have also taken batches.

B7RLE, like the B7TL and B9TL, is a more conventional chassis, with a vertical transverse engine. It is a heavyweight chassis designed for a 15+ year life. The engine is the D7E rated at 290bhp. B7RLE, like most chassis, is actually produced as two modules that are separated by the bodybuilder and then bodied to give a wheelbase of anything from 4.5m to 6.8m – in the UK and Ireland where the standard length is 12m overall.

The vast majority of chassis have been bodied by Wrights, the most notable exception being an order from Ulsterbus for schools traffic that was bodied by Alexander-Dennis to a high density seating configuration for 55. Plaxton, before being absorbed into the AD group, also produced a body for this chassis, with examples going to Blackpool and to Diamond Bus amongst others. MCV, an Egyptian based company with UK antecedents, successfully bodied two batches of B7RLE for Hong Kong and this body was offered, with a different specification to the Wright body, for the UK market in 2011. The stalwart Volvo operator Pulhams at Bourton-on-the-Water took three early examples, but, as with the B9TL double-deck body from this builder, supplies have been heavily interrupted by the political turmoil in the Middle East, especially Egypt in 2012 and 2013. MCV bodies, therefore, remain rare.

Over 2,000 chassis had been delivered in the UK and Ireland by the time production ceased in 2014.

Typical of the many hundreds of B7RLE/Wright delivered to First Group this example sits at Duns in the Scottish borders awaiting departure for Berwick-on-Tweed. To satisfy EU regulations the long route from Carlisle to Berwick has, technically, to be split at Duns. However, through ticketing is allowed and the bus, its passengers and driver all continue – only the destination display being changed! (RC)

Chassis diagram of B7RLE.

After the demise of the B10M it has been rare for Stagecoach to purchase new Volvo single-deck buses. The exception is the buses for the Cambridge Busway where two tranches of B7RLE/Wright have been placed in service – one of which is seen here. The other operator on the Busway, Whippet, also uses the B7RLE, initially with a small fleet of Plaxton-bodied vehicles that have now been replaced by Wright-bodied examples. (RC)

When Arriva gained the contract to operate the express service from Glasgow airport to Glasgow City Centre it purchased a fleet of 11 B7RLE/Wright painted in this striking variation of the Arriva livery. The purpose-built vehicles seated 37 and had a generous provision for luggage – the racking is visible through the first three window bays. (DC)

Yorkshire Coastliner had a small number of single-deck vehicles in its fleet to supplement the normal double-deck operation. This air conditioned example, seen at York en-route to Leeds, is one of six that joined the fleet in March 2005. Other companies in the Blazefield Group also took delivery of B7RLE/Wright at this time but to a slightly lower interior specification. (JAS)

163

Amongst the very varied fleet of CIE single-deck buses were 80 B7RLE/Wright delivered in 2008 and used across the whole system – and registered locally. This example is operating in Galway. Note the interesting panel over the second window bay used to promote a local festival. (MB)

A very early user of B7RLE was Rossendale who took eight vehicles in 2003. Route branding and extolling the virtues of low-floor vehicles was still very much in vogue. A striking new livery and Rosso fleetname is now in use. (HP)

Diamond Bus, part of the Rotala Group, is a keen user of B7RLE and has purchased both new and used examples. The fleet operating to the north of the West Midlands area is painted the dark blue shade shown here, but south of Birmingham, around Redditch, the livery is red. (DC)

164

In recent years Blackpool has been a rare purchaser of new buses. However, a small batch of Plaxton-bodied B7RLE, alongside some good used examples from the Blazefield Group, joined the fleet in 2006. The livery marked a striking departure from previous practice. Fleet number 526 is seen alongside one of Blackpool's modern trams. (DS)

Much is made of accessibility to modern public transport. This illustrates the ease with which wheelchair passengers, using integral and easily deployed ramps, can now board buses. Blackpool's new trams are equally user-friendly and the creation of bus-tram interchanges encourages the less mobile to travel by public transport. (DS)

A consistent purchaser of B7RLE has been Travel West Midlands. The example below left is seen working out of Wolverhampton to Codsall. Identical vehicles can be found in the National Travel outpost in Dundee, with only the fleetname to differentiate them. (DC)

In recognition of its isolation from the remainder of the West Midland network, National Travel uses a distinctive blue livery for its Coventry operation – inspired by the local football team. This is a 2013 delivery with a style of route branding that would be widely recognised. (DC)

165

Given the dominance of the state owned bus operator, relatively few independent companies in Eire invest in new service buses. One of the few is Suirway of Passage East in County Waterford who took delivery of this B7RLE in mid-2007. (MB)

By contrast, many UK independent operators will purchase or lease new vehicles, often for the initial duration of a tendered service. The B7RLE has proved a popular choice. Minsterley Motors in Shropshire have been consistently successful in tendering for supported services and have taken new B7RLE with both Plaxton and Wright bodies. This Plaxton-bodied example loads at Bishop's Castle. (MB)

Pulhams operate commercially from Cheltenham to their base at Bourton-on-the-Water and to Moreton-in-Marsh. This rare MCV-bodied vehicle, new in 2013, is one of a trio that have replaced long serving B10M and B12M coaches. Pulhams' vehicles are always impeccably turned out. (DC)

When Lothian Transport took over the services from Edinburgh to East Lothian abandoned by First Bus they established a separate operating company, using a distinctive livery and equipped with new B7RLE buses with Wright bodywork. This example, seen in Princess Street (with wiring for the Edinburgh trams system also in evidence) has worked one of the new services into Edinburgh. Typically, it is immaculately presented to the would-be passenger. (DC)

Lothian Transport has been a consistent purchaser of B7RLE for its single-deck needs. This well turned out 2004 vehicle, adorned with route branding, is in central Edinburgh in Princes Street. (DC)

First Bus, attempting to make part of the ex-Midland Red empire into a profitable operation, purchased B7RLE with Plaxton bodies from Viola, following the collapse of the Viola incursion into South Wales. This example is serving the famous 144 service linking Birmingham with Worcester. (DC)

167

The Volvo Olympian

The chassis enjoyed the rare distinction of being the only Volvo chassis sold with a name! Leyland had sold over 5,000 Olympians and overseas demand had led to Workington being kept open for twelve months longer than planned. The final deliveries from Workington were to Singapore, who ordered 200 chassis, and Hong Kong and to Strathclyde who urgently needed over 50 chassis to replace vehicles destroyed in the Larkfield fire. This was a legacy that had to be retained and developed.

Volvo's Olympian was to be built at Irvine and the chassis was considerably revised to take standard Volvo parts, partly to make spares holding easier and partly to reduce the cost of construction. Volvo achieved about 60% Volvo content. The main component was the Volvo TD102 engine, but also all the electrical systems were standard Volvo and the braking systems and hubs were to Volvo specification. The vehicle, therefore, looked, and sounded, like a Volvo. As a major concession to existing users Volvo continued to offer the Cummins engine as an option, but deleted Gardner from the option list – which may, incidentally, have been the final nail in the Gardner coffin. The Cummins option lasted until 1995 when Cummins ceased production of the L10 engine and replaced it with the physically larger M11 that would not comfortably fit into the Olympian engine bay. Thereafter the Volvo engine was the only option.

The new Olympian was well received and major orders were received from the home market, amongst them Stagecoach and Dublin Bus, both of whom made the Olympian their standard double-deck chassis. The decision by Dublin Bus to standardise on the Olympian chassis is an excellent example of the benefits to Volvo of the purchase of Leyland – prior to the takeover Volvo had tried without success to gain entry to the Dublin market. The Olympian also gave Volvo access to the London market. In 1993 Lothian Transport ordered 100 Olympian chassis. This was the largest double-deck chassis order in the UK for eight years and gives some idea of the very weak state of the market over the preceding years. As the market improved with the state of the economy, so Olympians penetrated all of the major groups.

The export market also brought in considerable business. Hong Kong operators, led by Citybus, were providing higher specification vehicles, including air conditioning in their tri-axle vehicles. The China Light and Power company purchased 15 Alexander-bodied vehicles to a very high coach specification using the vehicles to transport their workers. High specification vehicles are always more profitable than the standard specification, so these orders were doubly welcome. Singapore also continued its fleet renewal programme using the tri-axle Olympian chassis which it ordered in very large batches. The Olympian sold to every variety of customer in the UK and Ireland. Dublin alone took over 350 chassis, albeit with a Cummins engine, and at the other end of the scale small operators would purchase a single example at a time.

This happy state of affairs was ended by the European legislators, reinforced by the UK Parliament, who required disabled access to all forms of public transport. The step-entrance Olympian was not adaptable for this purpose, so a replacement had to be developed. Irvine, however, had produced over 5,000 Olympian chassis, exceeding the number produced by Leyland. The end of Olympian construction in 1999, ironically, also marked the end of production at the Irvine factory. The chassis was a great success by any measure. Many examples are still operating within all the major groups and many have been cascaded into the fleets of smaller operators where they continue to provide sterling service on school contracts and other forms of contracted service.

Despite the end of production in Irvine, and the ending of deliveries to the UK and Ireland, Olympian did live on for another five years in the lucrative Far Eastern export market as the B10TL-7300 – an updated tri-axle Olympian chassis sold exclusively in Hong Kong and to Singapore Bus Services. The last deliveries there did not take place until 2005 and these chassis are still giving excellent service. Alexanders bodied many, but not all, of these vehicles.

When Volvo first looked at the Olympian it was coded 5380. The first prototype Volvo chassis were, accordingly, numbered 5380/1 (the two axle prototype) and 5380/2 (the tri-axle prototype). Production at Irvine, however, ran from 25001 onwards. For the Leyland team there was a delightful irony in that at the launch of the Volvo Olympian chassis at Irvine, where the first chassis was still on the production line, the chassis available for inspection (25008) had been built previously at Farington.

A classical view of an Alexander-bodied Olympian. Working for Cumberland Motor Services it is on the lengthy Keswick to Lancaster route that traverses the heart of the English Lake District. (HP)

East Lancs provided the coachwork for many Olympians. Blue Bus of Horwich purchased several of this combination, two of which are pictured here in service in Wigan. Note the counter-intuitive fleet numbering! (MB)

Another operator who favoured the Olympian/East Lancs combination was Nottingham City Transport. This is a standard East Lancs body whereas many Nottingham vehicles carried the more distinctive Nottingham Style bodywork. (HP)

Blackpool, by contrast, favoured Northern Counties bodywork, represented here by a late Countybus style body and sporting the Metro livery that prevailed for many years in Blackpool. (HP)

169

Lancaster City Transport, one of the smaller but latterly more dynamic municipal operators, was given a new market with the advent of the University of Lancaster. Unable to afford new vehicles they purchased good, used stock. This is a Northern Counties-bodied Olympian that originated with Greater Manchester. (HP)

Finglands in Manchester also served a predominantly University market for which competition was intense. This Northern Counties-bodied Olympian is seen in Manchester Piccadilly competing with Stagecoach. That Finglands was a subsidiary of East Yorkshire is evident from the registration. (DC)

The Alexander-bodied Olympian became the standard purchase for Lothian Transport. The small amidship window is characteristic of the body when built on the long wheelbase chassis that was the normal purchase for this operator. (DC)

170

Not quite what it seems! The livery of this Alexander-bodied Olympian suggests that this bus should be working for Lancashire United. In fact, it has been transferred to Burnley and Pendle and is awaiting a repaint. This illustrates the problem that is created when vehicles are transferred within a group – in this case the very dynamic Blazefield Group – where each operating element has a distinctive livery. (HP)

Like Lothian Transport in Edinburgh, Dublin also had a large, standardised fleet of Olympians with Alexander bodywork. This 1999 delivery marked the last batch of Olympians. Dublin was the only major customer for the Olympian that year as rear-engined, low-floor vehicles rapidly became the norm – as was shortly to be the case in Dublin. (RC)

Bristol is a city that has long had a love/hate relationship with the internal combustion engine – whether in cars or buses. In an early attempt to resolve its ever increasing traffic problems the Long Ashton Park-and-Ride was introduced. Specially liveried Northern Counties-bodied Olympians were provided by Badgerline for this service. (DC)

171

Ipswich was an operator that had seriously considered purchasing the Ailsa, taking out an option for 15 underframes and then deciding that it would proceed no further. It was not surprising therefore, that this undertaking took Alexander-bodied Olympians into the fleet. The very traditional livery has a hint of modernity in the upsweep at the rear. (DC)

Delaine, at Bourne in Lincolnshire, had been a strong Leyland supporter. With the demise of that marque they slowly turned from an all Leyland fleet to an all Volvo fleet. An early part of this transition saw East Lancs-bodied Volvo Olympians enter service. This, rather empty, example heads back to the Bourne base. (PM)

Although the bulk of Stagecoach body orders went to Alexanders a significant number of Olympians for that company were bodied by Northern Counties. This example is with East Midland. The same combination could be found widely spread in England and notably in the London fleets of Stagecoach. (DC)

172

When First Group took over Strathclyde Transport it used overall red as a livery. With the strong lines of the Alexander body it was acceptable when new – as here – but once it had been dulled by the bus washer and received the odd scrape and dent it left much to be desired. Barbie was a great improvement. (DC)

The essentially rugged construction of the Olympian meant that it was still fit for service when the major operators removed it from front-line duties. This Northern Counties-bodied example began life with British Bus in London. It passed to Bee Line Buzz in Manchester and then moved to South Lancs Travel for use on school services. (MB)

Exports, especially to Hong Kong and Singapore, played a major role in the Olympian story. City Bus, an upstart newcomer to the Hong Kong bus scene, set new standards with their tri-axle Alexander-bodied Olympians that seated over 100 and gave the luxury of air conditioning. Kowloon Omnibus and China Motor Bus were soon forced to follow with their own examples of these impressive vehicles. This is an all-British example with an Irvine produced chassis and a Falkirk produced body, seen prior to shipment to Hong Kong. Later deliveries to Hong Kong featured chassis produced in Sweden and CKD bodies assembled locally. (MB)

B7TL Double-deck Chassis

Following the total failure of the B7L to make any headway as a double-deck chassis, Volvo was forced back to the drawing board to find an Olympian replacement. The need was urgent. Legislation was already in place that suggested the Olympian step entrance would be unacceptable within the life span of the chassis. Operators were already seeking a low-floor alternative. The prototype Dennis Trident was being shown to operators by late 1997 and the London market, especially, was demanding a low-floor product.

However easy it is to be wise after the event, Volvo did what they should probably have done earlier. They produced a more conventional rear-engined chassis with a transverse engine to a more conventional layout. The result was B7TL.

Unfortunately, the delays caused by the B7L débâcle meant that the B7TL was twelve months behind its Dennis competitor and this delay allowed the Guildford company to become a significant supplier of double-deck chassis. Dennis delivered vehicles from early 1999 and in the twelve months before Volvo caught up had delivered over 700 vehicles, mainly to the voracious and very significant London market. During 1999 Volvo had only the Olympian to offer and it was only large orders from Dublin that sustained Olympian production, a mere handful of chassis being delivered in the UK.

The early deliveries of B7TL in 2000 went to West Midlands and only slowly did Volvo penetrate the London market, mainly through early sales to the Go-Ahead Group. First Group and Arriva also became early customers as did some of the smaller groups such as Blazefield. Dual-sourcing, for whatever reason, became a policy in some fleets, thereby further reducing Volvo's grip in the market. Stagecoach, however, elected to stay with the Trident. Volvo's near dominance of the double-deck market had been broken and would never be regained.

B7TL was, however, a worthy successor to the Olympian. It was available in a variety of lengths, including, ironically, a 12-metre version on a tri-axle chassis, and the Volvo engine was already well proven in double-deck application in the Olympian. Bodywork was initially the Plaxton President – as with the ill fated B7L – produced at the ex-Northern Counties factory that was, by then, part of the Plaxton empire. Alexander and East Lancs also offered a body on this chassis from its inception. Wright bodywork was offered from 2001 and thereafter they became an increasingly significant supplier.

Travails, however, were not over for Volvo as the B7TL fell foul of noise emission regulations introduced in London and the last B7TLs were delivered to London – to London Central – in the first quarter of 2006. Production continued for 2006, with Dublin once again providing a major order to 'run out' the chassis. When deliveries of B7TL ceased at the end of 2006 over 4,400 chassis had been produced. The first 520 chassis were produced at the Irvine facility and then subsequently at Boras in Sweden. A small number of chassis went to non-British Isles destinations, notably a batch with Marco Polo bodies for Johannesburg.

An early user of the B7TL was West Midlands. Most were used in their conventional National Express Group colours but a small cohort, in a distinctive Airbus livery, was used on the Express Service to Birmingham Airport. This Plaxton-bodied example displays the livery to good effect. (DC)

Finglands, in Manchester, was another early user of the B7TL/Plaxton combination. This independent operator worked along the busy route serving the Universities to Didsbury in competition with Megabus and more conventional Stagecoach services. It is seen departing from Piccadilly. (DC)

All the major London operators purchased B7TL, many with Plaxton (later Transbus) bodies. This Metroline example, seen at North Finchley, sports the livery used by that company before the all red edict was issued by Transport for London. (TQ).

First Group's London livery was a variation on the willow leaf of the Barbie livery, combined with yellow panels flanking the destination box. Not the most elegant of liveries. (TQ)

Arriva was able to use a variation of the 'cow horn' for London, depicted here on an Alexander-bodied B7TL at Hampstead Heath. By the time this vehicle was built Alexander's, along with Plaxton, were part of the Transbus Group. (TQ)

175

London United had what many regarded as the most attractive of the London liveries and this Alexander-bodied B7TL, above, displays the then livery to good effect as it sits at Putney Bridge. Destination displays were rather more fulsome than at present. (TQ)

London United were also unusual in ordering East Lancs Vyking bodies for their B7TL operated in the capital city. One is seen below at Hammersmith bus station. By this time white had been eliminated from the livery and the body design gave a smaller destination display. (TQ)

176

The Blazefield Group services stretch across the Pennines operating from Manchester to the East Coast. The Group purchased many B7TL vehicles, mainly, but not exclusively, with Wright bodywork. The group's express services from the Lancashire towns into Manchester were skilfully branded and attained a high profile. Services ran regularly and quickly, using the motorway network where appropriate. This Lancashire Way liveried vehicle has entered Manchester at the lower end of Deansgate, having set out from Blackburn. (RC)

An early B7TL with Plaxton coachwork built at the old Northern Counties premises at Wigan make this Burnley and Pendle example almost a local product. Bound for Manchester it will have originated in Colne. The livery is the original Witch Way livery celebrating the mythical Pendle Witches. The Plaxton body would provide rather more comfort that a broomstick. (HP)

The success of the initial express services led to the rolling stock being upgraded, again with B7TL chassis, but this time with Wright bodywork and an upgraded livery. (RC)

177

B7TL found favour with Irish independent operators who often use double-deck vehicles for day tours and other sightseeing work. This coach-seated East Lancs-bodied example was new to Lally in County Galway in January 2004. Despite the claim on the front dash, it is a B7TL. (MB)

The old order changes! The major Irish user, indeed one of the major users, of B7TL was Dublin Bus. In the period from August 2000 to the end of 2006 almost 650, predominantly Alexander-bodied examples, entered service, replacing Olympians. The two generations are seen here in O'Connell Street. (MB)

Even in Ireland, notorious for rain, there is a market for open top vehicles. Here a well loaded East Lancs-bodied B7TL of Dualway, Rathcoole travels through Phoenix Park on a traditional City Sightseeing Tour. (MB)

178

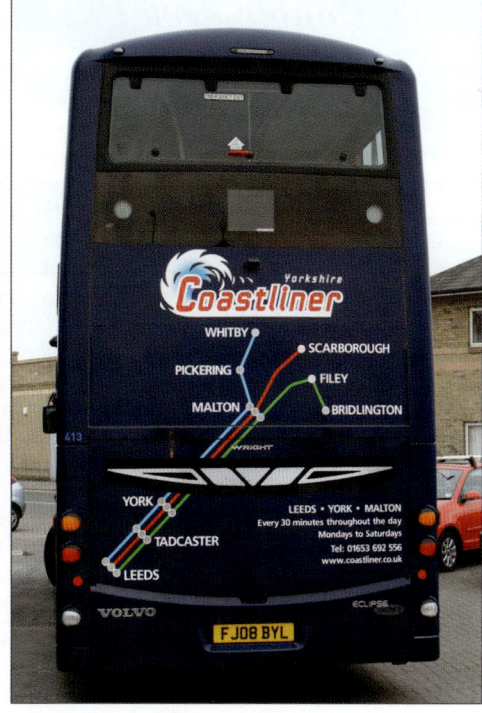

In contrast to the highly standardised fleet of Dublin Buses, Bus Eireann, the major state operator in Ireland, operates a very eclectic fleet. Amongst the variety are some 23 East Lancs-bodied B7TL finished to coach specification for express services into Dublin. This example, DD16 from the 2002 batch, arrives in O'Connell Street. Further examples followed in 2004. (RC)

Some operators are more imaginative than others! The Blazefield Group not only produced some very distinctive liveries for its main services in Lancashire and Yorkshire, it also used the rear of the bus to good effect. This Yorkshire Coastliner vehicle is awaiting its next duty at Malton depot and clearly displays the route network. Not surprisingly, Yorkshire Coastliner was the most profitable bus company in the UK for a number of years. (RC)

A very useful source of mid-life double-deck vehicles are operations in London. The major groups are able to cascade vehicles to their less arduous provincial operations. Go-Ahead has sent a large number of ex-London B7TL/East Lancs Mylennium-bodied vehicles to Plymouth, where it has given Citybus the capacity to compete with First Bus in, and around, the city. (KM)

179

B9TL Double-deck Chassis

B7TL was introduced in something of a hurry and although this was a successful chassis it had to have a number of modifications in its life time. These modifications and other improvements were introduced into a new double-deck chassis – the B9TL. This was intended to replace not only the B7TL but also, in the Far Eastern market, the Super Olympian.

B9TL introduced a new engine – D9B for the two-axle chassis and the more powerful D9A for the tri-axle chassis – and incorporated many of the lessons learned from operating B7TL, especially in London. B9TL was for some time offered only with Wright bodywork. This combination produced what was widely regarded as the best double-deck vehicle on the market. The result was orders from a very wide variety of operators in the UK and Ireland. Ireland – north and south – became a very important market with over 125 chassis going to Translink in Northern Ireland and almost 400 to Dublin and CIE. Dublin took an interesting batch of tri-axle vehicles with Alexander bodywork.

In the export market B9TL has been a resounding success. Almost 1,600 chassis operate in Singapore, nearly all with Wright bodywork. In Hong Kong most operators have taken delivery of batches of B9TL with a variety of bodywork – the Wright bodies established a precedent when they were locally assembled in China. Wright Bros, however, developed their own integral design and also offered a hybrid vehicle. Both of these products were to different specifications to the bodies supplied on Volvo chassis, but none-the-less they were in indirect competition with the Volvo products. An Egyptian based company, MCV, had roots in the UK and had successfully supplied bodywork on B7RLE to the demanding Hong Kong market.

In 2011, therefore, Volvo made an MCV body option available on B9TL, to a different specification to the Wright products. Volvo's timing was unfortunate, in that it coincided with major political upheavals in the Middle East and especially in Egypt where the MCV bodies were manufactured. MCV bodies on Volvo chassis, therefore, remain rare in the UK and non-existent in Ireland. With some deliveries still to be made in the Far East, around 5,000 chassis have been produced.

Typical of the large number of Wright-bodied B9TL delivered for use in London is this example with the Go-Ahead Group. It shows very clearly the smaller upper-deck side windows in bays 2 and 3 to accommodate the London specified air conditioning system. It is seen at Clapham Common Station. (TQ)

Even with edicts from Transport for London reducing scope for operator liveries, not all London buses are all-over red. The East London Transit subsidiary of Go-Ahead managed to introduce an element of individuality to this batch of B9TL. This example is in Ilford. (TQ)

180

For a time this was the only Egyptian-built MCV-bodied double-deck vehicle operating in the UK. The Go-Ahead Group B9TL is at Canning Town. Subsequently Golden Tours have taken examples for sightseeing work in London. Go-Ahead Group will take further MCV bodies in 2016, but mounted on B5LH chassis. (TQ)

Bus Eireann took a number of B9TL vehicles for service in the provinces. This example, with Wright bodywork, in provincial livery and carrying a local registration, is operating in Cork. (MB)

Lothian Transport have been enthusiastic users of B9TL. A small batch was delivered with very high specification interiors and a very distinctive livery for use on the airport shuttle service. Two examples await departure from Waverley Bridge in Edinburgh. (DC)

181

Ulsterbus made the Volvo/Wright combination the standard double-deck vehicle in the province. This example is on Olympic Games Duty in London in 2012. It was a great pity that Transport for London insisted that all identification had to be removed for this work as many operators were proud to contribute to the event. (DC)

An indulgence. A Bus Vannin B9TL visited the Jurby Transport Museum of the Manx Transport Trust before entering service. It is seen here alongside a 1927 Leyland Lion that began life with Road Services in the Isle of Man. Bus design has moved a long way in the intervening period. The Lion is now undergoing restoration in the workshops of Bus Vannin. (RC)

Dublin Bus operates several services from Dublin Airport to the City. The 748 is an express service that terminates at Heuston Railway Station, giving connection, by rail, to the West of the country. The picture is at Heuston station. (RC)

182

First Group were the single largest user of B9TL/ Wright vehicles and they entered most of the First Group fleets. Here a First Manchester example sports a rather feeble route branding modification to the standard Barbie livery for the service from Manchester to Bolton that compares poorly with the Blazefield Groups branding for similar services (see p 177) (JAS)

A Stagecoach operated B9TL/ Wright seems improbable, but when Stagecoach took-over some First Group services in North Manchester they acquired several examples. Although branded for Stagecoach this example has not been repainted. The batch of vehicles were quickly moved to Scotland. (DC)

This Wright-bodied vehicle is with Yorkshire Coastliner. Operating from a main depot at Malton the company runs express services from Leeds to various points on the Yorkshire Coast. All the vehicles are to a high interior specification and carry this very distinctive livery. (RC)

183

Dublin Bus took the issue of moving crowds seriously and introduced a large batch of tri-axle B9TL with Alexander bodywork. This picture emphasises the length of these vehicles – and their traffic blocking potential! (MB)

In the UK East Lancs bodied a number of tri-axle, 100-seat, B9TL. They are popular with operators as they can carry three school classes with ease, or large parties wanting to travel relatively short distances. Weaverway took the initial three, and one of this trio has migrated North to Tyrer in Lancashire. (MB)

Arriva, owners of the Original London Sightseeing Tour, have taken B9TL with both fully open top and part-open top bodies by Optare. This part-open top example, seen pulling away from Victoria Railway Station, seems to be better suited to the English climate. (TQ)

184

B5LH Double-deck Bus Chassis

If ever there was a 'political bus' this is it! In the 1990s and early years of the new Millennium, the environment rose rapidly up the European political agenda. With it went a debate on the value of clean air in cities and a determination by European political leaders to improve air quality in cities and more widely. This concern, along with the already articulated desire to reduce carbon emission in order to reduce global warming, led inexorably towards electric drive and propulsion systems as well as low carbon emission engines, culminating in the Euro 6 regulations.

The most practical result to date has been the hybrid bus, using a low emission diesel engine to charge batteries that drive the vehicle in certain modes – start up and slow speed – which then cuts in to drive the bus directly.

The hybrid power B5LH was developed in response to this political demand. Hybrid technology is complex and expensive and the resulting vehicle is about 33% more expensive than a conventional diesel powered bus. This is a very expensive way of reducing emissions in inner city areas and other places, such as the Mersey tunnels, where it was deemed necessary to improve air quality. Although hybrid vehicles are more fuel efficient than their non-hybrid counterparts, neither Volvo, nor any of their competitors, have reached the point where hybrid technology is commercially viable.

Commercially the hybrid bus does not make sense in the current 'state of the art', and, with only relatively small numbers being purchased for specific applications, the price reduction that might result from larger production runs has yet to happen – a situation not helped by the presence of four competitors in the very small market. The only way in which hybrid buses have been purchased in the UK is by a direct subsidy from the Government. One benefit from hybrid technology is that the diesel engine used is smaller than would normally be required resulting in lower fuel consumption. Fuel saving appears to be about 30%, no matter which form of the technology is used. It is not unusual, therefore, to find vehicles purchased for high intensity, inner city, weekday services in more remote parts of operators' systems at the weekends. The 'elephant in the room' for which no-one seems yet to have formulated a definitive answer, is how much a set of replacement batteries will cost.

Volvo's B5LH uses a parallel drive system in which the diesel engine cuts out completely when the vehicle is stationary and uses the electric power to move away from a stop – a completely silent operation, not unlike a trolleybus from days of yore. At a predetermined speed the diesel engine cuts in to assist the electric motor and then ultimately takes over completely. The 'direct drive' mode means that the B5LH has a much greater ability to run at higher speeds than the competing products – an important consideration on inter-urban services. The parallel drive system also means that should the electric drive fail the bus can be driven using the diesel engine alone.

B5LH was available initially only with Wright bodywork and has been purchased by most of the major groups and a few,

Transport for London is the largest user of hybrid vehicles, having several hundred in service. This example of the B5LH shows the line of the Wright bodywork well. The very subdued hybrid logo used by TfL contrasts with the more exotic liveries used by other operators to designate hybrid vehicles and to announce their green credentials. (TQ)

West Midlands also operate B5LH with standard Wright body. The livery here is much more interesting and proclaims 'green-ness' with great exuberance. (DC)

185

intrepid independent operators such as Bakers at Biddulph and Bullocks in Manchester. In 2014 Stagecoach took their first B5LH with Wright bodies – a batch of 30 for London. In conjunction with Volvo, Wrights have taken a considerable amount of weight out of the Gemini body – producing the Gemini 3 body that will weigh around,10,000 Kg depending on specification – a useful drop of over 1000 Kg that enables more passengers to be carried.

In 2014 Volvo announced a revival of their relationship with Alexander, resulting in orders for the B5LH with Alexander bodywork from both Stagecoach and the Go-Ahead group.

Many of the B5LH vehicles have been supplied with a full contract maintenance package. Arriva, one of the early purchasers of B5LH – a group that subsequently operated other hybrid products – has pronounced that the B5LH is the most reliable of the hybrid products.

A delightful irony is that 40 years after Ailsa Bus unsuccessfully sought to produce a low-height Ailsa underframe, Wrights have produced a low-height B5LH design and the first examples entered service with The Oxford Bus Company in late 2013.

First Group operate the B5LH in a number of urban environments. A variation on the Barbie livery is used to good effect. This example is seen in central Leeds. (JAS)

Arriva have been firm supporters of the B5LH and purchased them for both their London and provincial operations. As one of the few operators to use all three makes of hybrid bus available in the UK – Alexander-Dennis, Wright and Volvo – it is significant that they have found the B5LH to be the most reliable. The striking livery on this North West based vehicle is an interesting interpretation of the original 'cow horn' style.(DC)

186

Very few small operators use hybrid technology. One of that small band was Bakers at Biddulph in Staffordshire who used their three B5LH on the lengthy route from Stafford to Stoke-on-Trent. The higher speed capability of the B5LH was well used on this inter-urban service. One of the trio displays its prominent branding and slogans in this view. *(RC)*

Amongst the more esoteric liveries on B5LH is this very striking design used by Go-Ahead North East for its branded service from Newcastle to Low Fell, passing the iconic Angel of the North. *(Go-North East) (DC)*

Go-Ahead also operates B5LH in London but to the dual-door London specification. This example is seen in Whitehall heading for the legendary Elephant and Castle. *(TQ)*

187

7900 Hybrid Single-deck Bus

This is the single-deck version of the B5LH double-deck vehicle. Mechanically it is very similar to the B5LH using the same D5F engine, rated at 215bhp. The bus comes as a complete vehicle with Volvo coachwork produced in Poland – it is not, despite some opinions to the contrary, an integral vehicle. The 7900 is the second generation of hybrid single-deck vehicle to be offered by Volvo in Europe – the UK market was deemed to be too small for the first generation to be re-engineered for right hand drive.

As with the B5LH double-deck bus in the UK, the 7900 has found some favour in Europe with those operators seeking an inter-urban capability, but this has yet to emerge as a market in Great Britain.

Like the B5LH, the 7900 is considerably more expensive than its diesel counterpart and is dependent upon a grant regime for purchase in the UK. Offered there only from 2013 onwards it has been operated enthusiastically by Lothian with 50 in service and further examples on order, and by First Group.

Lothian transport have proved to be firm supporters of the 7900, having taken the first examples in the UK and subsequently placed two follow-on orders. 2016 will see a further contingent delivered with an overhead charging facility. The Lothian livery makes these vehicles look most attractive. (PC)

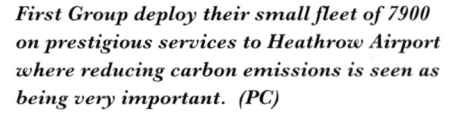

First Group deploy their small fleet of 7900 on prestigious services to Heathrow Airport where reducing carbon emissions is seen as being very important. (PC)

First Essex also has a small fleet of 7900 which operate in this attractive variation on First Group livery around Chelmsford. (PC)

188

Chapter 4
Euro 6

In theory January 1st 2014 saw the implementation of the Euro 6 emission controls. These are stricter than anything that has preceded it and require major improvements in engine emissions. Volvo have determined that this requires a new range of engines rather than trying to squeeze new life out of older designs.

Three engines will be used to cover the range of power requirements that Volvo foresee for the immediate future. These are a 5-litre engine, the D5K, an 8-litre engine, the D8K, and an 11-litre engine, D11K. These engines will be available in the UK with a range of power outputs to meet the various needs of operators.

The Euro 6 model line-up will be:

- B8R   this chassis will replace both the B7R and the B9R as a coach chassis. It will have the 8-litre engine available in power outputs of 280, 320 and 350bhp.
- B11R   this coach chassis, in two-axle and three-axle form, will replace the B13R chassis, using the new 11-litre engine at power outputs ranging from 380bhp to 460bhp. It is anticipated that a number of B9R operators will switch to this chassis as well as B13R users. This chassis will also form the basis for the 9700 coach with Polish-built Volvo coachwork.
- B8RLE   this will replace the popular and long running B7RLE bus chassis. This chassis will also use the same 8-litre engine as the B8R coach chassis.
- 7900H   the hybrid single-deck bus sold as a complete unit with Polish-built bodywork and using the new, 5-litre engine and the same propulsion system as the B5LH double-deck chassis.
- B5TL   this double-deck chassis will replace the B9TL. It will, counter-intuitively, use the new, 4-cylinder, 5-litre engine rated at 240bhp in most UK operations. Plans to fit the 8-litre engine were dropped when the performance of the 5-litre unit was evaluated.
- B5LH   this double-deck, hybrid, chassis will continue into the Euro 6 era. It will use the same engine as the B5TL diesel only chassis and the same driveline as the 7900 single-deck bus.

For the UK market the preferred bodybuilder partners for the Euro 6 era are:
for bus application – Wright, with MCV and Alexander (AD) as associate builders
for coach application – Plaxton, with Jonckheere, Sunsundegui, and Caetano as associate builders.

Euro 6 engines are more complex than their predecessors and there was an initial expectation that fuel consumption might suffer, but this appears not to be the case. Improvements in fuel consumption are proving to be well in advance of Euro 5. Ironically, at a time when fuel prices are a major concern to operators all over Europe, the EU regulations that encompass Euro 6 are only concerned with engine emissions, not with fuel consumption. Because of the radical change that Euro-6 brings to the engineering, and the rise in cost associated with this, including the cost of retraining for fleet engineers, it was anticipated that initial purchases of Euro 6 would be 'slow' – reflecting a desire by many operators to acquire as many new Euro 5 vehicles as possible before the 31st December 2013 deadline.

The Euro 6 deadline however, has proved to be more flexible than was originally thought. The UK coalition Government, despite ostensibly having concerns for the environment, failed to pass the necessary enabling legislation through the UK Parliament. There was provision within the European legislation for 'small batches' – up to 1,000 vehicles – to be sold within Europe. This 'loophole' has enabled UK operators to continue to place in service Euro 5 vehicles – a provision the major groups and some of their suppliers adopted enthusiastically. It would now seem likely that it will be 2016 before all UK deliveries are to Euro 6 standard as manufacturers will no longer hold 'derogated' stock.

In the Republic of Ireland a different situation has prevailed with appropriate legislation in place. Volvo has been very successful in placing Euro 6 vehicles in service. B11R has been especially successful in the coaching field and Bus Eireann has a large number of B5TL being delivered. A similar situation arises in Northern Ireland.

Volvo was able to supply a limited number of Euro 5 chassis to the UK market in 2014 and early 2015 – limited by the ability of Sweden to supply Euro 5 chassis. Euro 6 chassis, as predicted, sold 'slowly but surely' as operators gained experience of the new engines and associated systems.

A Volvo Leopard seems incredible! To coincide with the introduction of Euro 6 Plaxton introduced a new coach body, the Leopard, to go with the B8R or B11R chassis. (RC)

Displayed at Bus and Coach Live in October 2014 this Euro 6 B11R-based Plaxton Elitei was an early Euro 6 delivery to Matthews at Inesskeen in County Monaghan. It was also the first Elitei delivered to an independent operator. (MB)

Aircoach has taken delivery of a batch of B11R with the new Plaxton Leopard coachwork for their developing links to Dublin Airport. This example is on service from Cork to Dublin. Aircoach trialled the prototype Caetano-bodied B11R before deciding on Plaxton coachwork. (MB)

Volvo's own Polish-built coachwork has found considerable favour in Ireland, especially amongst operators of express services set-up in competition with Bus Eireann. This B11R-chassied example is operating for Go-Bus from Galway to Dublin Airport. (MB)

The B5TL/Wright combination has found favour with Bus Eireann for its double-deck fleet, both in Dublin and in the provinces. This example is in Cork. (MB)

Matthews have continued to purchase the Euro 6 compliant B11R/Plaxton combination. Slightly less exotic than the Elitei, the air conditioned Plaxton Leopard coachwork provides an excellent vehicle for the company's touring programme. (MB)

In England during 2014 delivery of Euro 6 models was slow, as, like its competitors, Volvo also supplied Euro 5 compliant models. Deliveries of Euro 6 models to operators such as Steels marked an increasing acceptance of the new technology. (DC)

191

Chapter 5
The End Of The Road – Rust, Rescue, Restoration

After 15 to 20 years of hard work, buses and coaches become too expensive to maintain economically and it becomes cheaper to replace them. The usual fate of old vehicles is that they pass to an 'End of Vehicle Life' specialist – ie a scrapyard – and are broken up with some parts salvaged for further use and the remainder turned into the proverbial razor blades. It is rare now that a vehicle passes to a showman or becomes a mobile shop.

Some operators, however, find a further use for vehicles as seat stores or places to keep those parts that 'just might be useful one day'. In some parts of the UK the scrap value of a vehicle does not warrant the cost of taking it to a scrap yard, so vehicles are just put in to a field or the bottom of the yard and left to quietly decay. Less frequently, a vehicle simply ceases to be used and is kept in a garage only to emerge when the operator changes hands or ceases to trade – these are the vehicles beloved of preservationists.

In areas where there is little scrap value in a life-expired coach they may be simply parked-up and left to rot – and to receive the attention of the local vandals. This Plaxton-bodied B58 was delivered to Georgeson and Moore on Scalloway in July 1980 and spent its whole working life serving this remote island community. Doubtless, usable mechanical parts have already been removed. (MB)

The B7L/Plaxton demonstrator sits forlornly in a Cheshire dealers yard in 2013. For many years it 'lay around' the Plaxton factory and then went to Manchester Technical College where it was used to demonstrate the independent front suspension. It was never registered and never used in revenue earning service. An interesting preservation project. (See page 156) (RC)

Splendidly restored by the 4738 Group ex-London Transport Ailsa V1 has been restored in the Leaside Buses livery that it originally acquired when based at Potters Bar. The 4738 Group has also restored three other Ailsas, including Derby's low-height example, and has one more possible candidate for restoration. (DC)